COMMENTARIES
On
A COURSE IN MIRACLES

TARA SINGH

Commentaries

—————————— *On* ——

A
COURSE
IN
MIRACLES

FOUNDATION FOR LIFE ACTION
Los Angeles

Library of Congress Cataloging in Publication Data
Singh, Tara, 1919-
Commentaries on A course in miracles.

Bibliography: p.
1. Foundation for Inner Peace. Course in miracles.
2. Spiritual life. I. Title.
BP610.S5612 1986   299'.93   86-18350
ISBN 1-55531-015-X Limited Edition, Hardbound
ISBN 1-55531-016-8 Softcover

*I am indebted to Lucille Frappier for her long
hours of devoted work. Without her assistance,
this book would not have been possible.*

*I am also grateful to the following friends for their help
in the preparation of this book: Aliana Scurlock, Jim
Cheatham, Johanna Macdonald, Charles Johnson,
Norah Ryan, Sandra Lewis, Clio Dixon, Frank Nader,
Kris Heagh, Connie Willcuts and John Williams.*

Contents

CONTENTS

*Poems from *The Gifts Of God* by the scribe
of *A Course In Miracles*.

Introduction

Man's real work is unselfish,
hence non-commercial.
It is not labor, but effortless —
independent of insecurity and doubt.

Men who live by beliefs and concepts
do not have a mind of their own,
nor have they as yet heard their own direct Voice.

To the Wise who lives by FACT,
feelings, reactions, opinions and beliefs
have no reality whatsoever.

How rare is the gift of True Knowledge
which questions the programmed existence
of man on earth.
It liberates those who would heed —
who, by heeding the direct Voice,
are set free of their conclusions.

A Course In Miracles[1] is a great gift to mankind
for we now have the Absolute amidst the relative.

This book, *Commentaries On A Course In Miracles*,
emerged out of the tuition-free One Year Retreat.
The One Year Retreat contributed these gifts:

— Non-Commercialized Action
— Self-Reliance
    and
— A Life Free of Consequences.

In present society,
where the monetary system is in control,
is it possible to step out and come to Self-Reliance?
Self-Reliance and a Life Free of Consequences
are almost inconceivable.
They go contrary to everything
man is educated to believe.
Self-Reliance is a way of life
that is totally lost in a world of appetites.

Mr. J. Krishnamurti has said,

"Society will not change,
yet the human being can."

But where would he start;
how would he implement it?
It is like stepping out of time.
The energy would have to be of one's own virtue
to be part of such an action.

Self-Reliance is independent of the externals.
It is not even part
of the present thought system of man.
It is of the Will of God — free of opposites.
To succeed in realizing the authenticity of it
is an internal action.
To merit it requires impeccable integrity —
the ethics that you would not compromise,
for you do not seek success
but virtue and self-honesty.

Then one may qualify for higher laws
whose wisdom sustains creation.
Unless it is an extension of Divine Laws,
it is not Self-Reliance.
Self-Reliance would not be dependent
on charity or donations,
nor can the money of false work support it.

Since man has lost his work,
he has become subject to jobs.
Now he must find his own inner calling
and come to intrinsic work.
The Foundation for Life Action
is dedicated to Rightness
which has its own strength
and will not adopt wrong means to justify right ends.
Gratefulness is its first principle.
It is not here to accomplish anything,
for it is intrinsic —
an expression of fulfillment, not ambition.
Those who represent the Foundation
are those to whom God is their first love.

Responsibility is the highest sensitivity;
its pure energy is impersonal.
Selfless work takes away the sense of insecurity.
Gratefulness is the solution to all problems.

If you can be fully grateful then you can receive
without being hindered by doubt or illusions.
of personal gain, loss or self-improvement.
Gratefulness is the praise of a pure heart.
Its light undoes illusions.
It is untouched by anything of the earth.

Having received the pure energy of Gratefulness,
you live by:

> *I am here only to be truly helpful.*
> *I am here to represent Him Who sent me . . . .*
> *I am content to be wherever He wishes. . .*[2]

and see the world through His eyes.

The Foundation was started with no money
but it had the conviction
not to seek or live off donations.
It offers the intimate atmosphere
of one-to-one relationship
and provides a productive life of intrinsic work
where one is awakened to Self-Reliance
by having something of one's own to give.
Productive life is essential for happiness and peace.

> Love has its own Divine Intelligence.
> Truth and Rightness are fully protected.
> Man needs to be in harmony with the Absolute —
> the highest Good, Love and Beauty.
> It is the human spirit
> that transcends the externals
> and realizes:

> "I AM THAT I AM."

Non-Commercialized Life is an internal action.
It demonstrates to the world that it is possible
to reverse the process of dependence
and irresponsibility.

*   *   *

In September, 1985, the School —
"Having the Ears to Hear"[3] —

situated at *The Branching of the Road*,[4] evolved
out of the Non-Commercialized Retreat,
now in its fourth year.
Its purpose is to train teachers
to bring *A Course In Miracles* into application.

The School is based on:

— Having one's own intrinsic work
    and not working for another.
— Being self-reliant and living
    a non-commercial life.
— Never taking advantage of another.
— Gratefulness.
    and
— Having to give what St. Peter gave.

    ''Silver and gold have I none;
    but such as I have give I thee.''[5]

The School is dedicated to a JUST life.

JUST is of True Knowledge
consistent with the Absolute.
Free from ''me and mine,''
it is impersonal.
JUST is an awakening,
not learned but received.
It brings Divine Order into one's life.

What is JUST is always consistent
for it is not subject to time.
It is related to the eternal laws of creation.
To be JUST, man has to relate with Facts.
A Fact cannot be interpreted.
It is ''What Is'' and awakens one
from the sleep of illusion.

The facts we know are of physical senses
and physical science.
But Reality is beyond relative knowledge.
Only Absolute Knowledge knows the Truth.
The originality of a Fact — the power of it —
transforms man's life.
To know a Fact is to have its strength.

Because the Name of God cannot be commercialized
and ill-earned money begets other vices,
the School charges no tuition.
We have no external goals nor sense of lack.

Real welfare lies in using things properly.
Wrong use of money brings misfortune.
Expenditure of funds is to be
exactly for the purpose for which it is entrusted.
Property and wealth are valueless
compared to contentment.
The Course advises us to stay free of entanglements
and to honor:

> *I will not value what is valueless.*[6]

The School is for those who realize:

> The Course is to be lived
> and bringing it into application
> is the obvious next step.

A Course In Miracles states:

> *When you come to the place where the branch
> in the road is quite apparent, you cannot go
> ahead. You must go either one way or the
> other. For now if you go straight ahead, the
> way you went before you reached the branch,
> you will go nowhere. The whole purpose of*

*coming this far was to decide which branch you
will take now. The way you came no longer
matters. It can no longer serve. No one who
reaches this far can make the wrong decision,
although he can delay. And there is no part of
the journey that seems more hopeless and futile
than standing where the road branches, and
not deciding on which way to go.* [7]

It was the sincere yearning in man
that brought *A Course In Miracles,*
with its step-by-step curriculum, into manifestation.
Similarly, this School exists for those
who long to give themselves to a new lifestyle.
It is a school where you come not to *learn,* but to *be.*

Without the space of the one-to-one relationship,
it would not have been possible for the Foundation
to evolve as a school to assist students
in coming to self-reliance
and having something of their own to give.

The Scribe of *A Course In Miracles* said to me directly:

"The Course is to be lived."

Non-Commercialized Action,
Self-Reliance
and a Life Free of Consequences

are the gifts of *A Course In Miracles.*

*Spirit is in a state of grace forever.
Your reality is only Spirit.
Therefore you are in a state of grace forever.* [8]

Knowing that man is Spirit,
the Wise extends only love —

the indivisible light of the Will of God.
He is ever a stranger to doubt and despair
and never sells True Knowledge.
This is the premise of Non-Commercialized Life.

No one can purchase True Knowledge
which is Just and Sacred.
For it is accessible only to those
who have the ears to hear
and the capacity to receive.

The purpose of these Commentaries
is to help remove,
as *A Course In Miracles* states:

> . . . *the blocks to the awareness*
> *of love's presence.* . .[9]

Statement of the Participants
Of The
One Year Non-Commercialized Retreat

As students of *A Course In Miracles,*
we are the disciples of the One
in charge of Atonement.
He is to us — Alive.
We think with Him.
Whatever we do, is done by — Him.

Ours is the Ministry of Gratefulness.
Together, productive and self-reliant,
we stand on our own feet
to bring the Course into application in our lives
and prepare to see man, in Truth,
as the Altar of God on Earth.
And extend to the tired world,
taxed by meaningless work,
the message of — Fulfillment.

We have no projects,
no ambition to own a community,
or external ashrams.
We do not commercialize life,
nor ask for donations.

Our own sincerity and purity of work
makes our life intrinsic.
We are strengthened by the power
of seeing a — Fact,

and the integrity of single purpose.
We do not work for another
and see no man contaminated by external unreality.

We have found our — Calling,
having heard the whisper of Absolute Knowledge.
Gratefulness, Forgiveness,
Non-attachment are — Real.
And fulfillment already is a part of — Love.

IN GOD WE TRUST.

Our lesson for today is:

My mind is part of God's.
I am very holy.[10]

Part 1

Anniversary

A year is short. Yet given unto Me
It lasts forever. Every minute is
Encased in silver; every hour in gold.
The months are splashed with stars, and they become
A diadem the angels will preserve
In shining brightness as your gift to Me.

It gains in glory every day it waits
For your returning. And the love in which
You gave it waits as well. My gratitude
Shines on its star points, polished carefully
By angels' wings, and kept immaculate
Against the time I give it back to you.[1]

This poem is from *The Gifts Of God* by the scribe of *A Course In Miracles*. It is an incomparable book of poetry containing some of the most important words ever spoken.

CHAPTER 1

Basic Premise Of
A COURSE IN MIRACLES

*All that stands between you and the power of
God in you is but your learning of the false.
. . . Be willing, then, for all of it to be undone.²*

A *COURSE IN MIRACLES* is not a learning. It is an undoing. It questions
everything we think we know.

This is revolutionary and quite a challenge.
Why? Because we live in a world of attachment, a
world of ideas and beliefs. This is self-destructive at
the national level as well as at the individual level.
We think we are American, Chinese, Christian,
Moslem, communist, capitalist, and so on. And I
wonder if anyone has ever questioned the abstract
ideas of division in which man is caught. There is
contradiction, conflict and constant duality within
us. This is a fact and no amount of learning will
bring us to the clarity in which this conflict ends.

*Nothing you have ever learned can help you
understand the present, or teach you how to*

undo the past. Your past is what you have taught yourself. Let it all go. . . . Your part is very simple. You need only recognize that everything you learned you do not want.[3]

We can see that *A Course In Miracles* is a process of undoing what we already know rather than of accumulating more. We already know too much. And all our learning and knowing has not affected our selfishness or our greed and insecurity. Have we learned to be self-reliant? Have we learned never to be confused, without contradictions in our life? If we have, then I would say we have learned something. But what we call learning is just an indulgence because it does not relate us to the reality that we are.

This, personality cannot learn. Personality gets lonely, bored, and insecure and then gets into the activity of self-improvement. It doesn't question: ''Is self-improvement necessary?'' The need of improving who you *are* is an assumption, you see. If we are already perfect — created in the image of God — then the process of self-improvement is an indulgence.

In ancient times, when parents wanted their child to learn a craft or skill, they sent him to a teacher or to a school. But if they wanted him to learn about life, they would take the child to a wise person, a sage, a saint. This saint, knowing truth directly, did not preach someone else's words or someone else's thoughts. He had nothing to teach. He awakened the child to his own potential, to his own perfection.

We avoid the discovery of our own perfection

and in the absence of that, we think someone else is going to give it to us or that someone else knows more than we do.

What is perfection? If I tell you, then you will be relying on my words. We do not want to come to perfection — we want perfection *described*. There are people who write books about it and the echoes go on and on. Most of these people are mere interpreters of knowledge, not men of direct knowing. We avoid the man of direct knowing because he represents a challenge. He will want you to let go of your belief systems which are borrowed and to which you give so much authority.

The wise person is simple and at peace. He is finished with learning; he has seen that our knowings — actually "educated ignorance" — deprive us of innocence. The state of innocence is alive and energetic, and never touched by deception. When will our learning come to an end so that we discover what innocence has to unfold?

A Course In Miracles awakens us, undoes our conclusions and questions our belief systems. It endeavors to free us from our concept of self. (Freedom is only freedom from self. It is not something bestowed upon man by a constitution.) What a state of being it must be that has no duality in it! And without knowing this, learning has no validity; it is a preoccupation with survival; it does not bring man closer to his peace.

See that in your own life learning and ideas have not helped. What is abstract can only keep you away from your own vitality. The knowledge that personality acquires through books and gurus promotes separation. It gives you concepts and lofty ideals and better skills, but greed is still greed and the inner conflict remains.

The state of innocence introduces one to the Love that is independent. What is independent extends what it is. It is not subject to conditions, pressures and circumstances. Love teaches effortlessly for it has its own vitality to extend. It is creative. Because no one is outside of it there are no judgments in it, and one is finished with the idiosyncrasies of likes and dislikes. This is what it means to be awakened.

> Love is one. It has no separate parts and no degrees; no kinds or levels, no divergencies and no distinctions. It is like itself, unchanged throughout. It never alters with a person or a circumstance. It is the heart of God, and also of His Son.[4]

A Course In Miracles makes certain things very clear. It states that there is One Mind — the Mind of God — of which we are all a part. Knowing this as truth ends duality. When you are not awakened to this truth, then you are with the personality mind that is self-centered, concerned about body needs and limited to the human thought system.

The mind of man, the personality mind, is constantly changing, selecting, choosing better circumstances. It is always in turmoil because it cannot find peace. In the mind of the personality — on which religions, universities and politics are built — there are constant changes. Nations and individuals seek to be at a point of advantage. When you seek advantage, it is always over someone else, and therefore, loveless. These are things we have to know.

The thought system of man promotes separation and how to be comfortable or better than someone else in separation. Learning assumes quite an importance but in reality has very little validity. It has not civilized man. It has done nothing to improve him.

In this separation there is the isolation of belief systems and no direct relationships. In fact, there is no relationship at all. What we call relationship, according to the thought system of man, is dependence. Sometimes you may be satisfied with the dependence; other times you may want to change it.

And what is the definition of the Mind of God? It does not change. That is relationship.

A Course In Miracles, as we have said, deals with the undoing and the questioning of the manmade world. From the very outset it says:

> *Nothing real can be threatened.*
> *Nothing unreal exists.*[5]

This is its premise. The world of reality is the world of unity that relates one to Eternal Laws. All the forces of the universe are focused in man. Man is the greatest of all flowering in the universe. Even the planets are subject to him. And in order to relate him to his own vastness, the Course undoes his misperceptions. This very undoing itself begins to relate him to other potentials within himself.

To see the fallacy of misperceptions demands the urgency of one who feels the pain of separation and wants to come to wholeness. Therefore, he no longer projects activity or pursues distractions. He questions everything. There is vitality.

What then is urgency? Urgency dissolves all deceptions. Urgency brings man to an awareness where the learning ceases and actuality is. We think seeing faults in other people is awareness. But that is merely looking with opinion through sightless eyes. In awareness, there is no separation for it has the purity of innocence.

What constitutes innocence? Innocence is not contaminated by the so-called learning of self-survival and the commotion of personality. In simple terms, it means that there is either Action, which is of Life, creative and impersonal, or there is the activity of personality in which we deny ourselves the creative action.

Mankind is becoming busier and busier. Activity is increasing. Yet the man of action is independent of activity. He is an extension, not an idiosyncrasy. He never doubts himself. He makes sure that nothing of the outside intrudes upon that extension because it is of love and perfection, ever in harmony with creation.

To the degree that man is weak, he begins to depend on the authority of corporations, governments or religious leaders to make decisions. Belief in someone else's authority promotes dependence and acknowledges inferiority. It undermines the individual. This dependence on external authority has hampered man's ability to call upon his full potentials and discover truth directly.

But are you interested in truth? If you are sincere, you must outgrow deception. This is what true religion is. It is not a dogma nor a belief system. A religious person is one who lives without being false.

A Course In Miracles dissolves thoughts, concepts and the preoccupations of the personality. It brings you to the State itself — to the Mind of God. It does not establish another religion.

As you begin to awaken, you harness the energy inherent in each day's lesson to bring you to the application of its truth.

Today, as it has been throughout the ages, the difficulty lies in application. We know that peace is good; we know we should love; we know we should not tell lies. But our knowledge does not bring us to application. We can learn a lot and still live contrary to what we learn.

We are caught in a lifestyle of compromise. It has us in its grip. We have very little idea of what wisdom, simplicity or innocence are. We are busy, worn out people. Our very lifestyle is self-destructive. And the application of the Course demands a change of lifestyle.

The daily lesson introduces man to the Path of Virtue related with Eternal Laws rather than man-made rules. When you relate with Eternal Laws, you can no longer fit into a meaningless, pressured existence.

Your holiness reverses all the laws of the world. It is beyond restriction of time, space, distance and limits of any kind. Your holiness is totally unlimited in its power because it establishes you as a Son of God, at one with the Mind of His Creator.

Through your holiness the power of God is made manifest. Through your holiness the power of God is made available. And there is nothing the power of God cannot do.[6]

CHAPTER 2

A COURSE IN MIRACLES
How It Came About

How did *A Course In Miracles* come into being? Why did it come? These are questions every person could ask. But in order to know what is real one would have to know laws that are universal and eternal; one would have to be independent of curiosity, independent of just wanting to know information.

Laws cannot be known through relative knowledge. Relative knowledge can give you the details of its history, but that kind of knowledge means very little. The difficulty is always the same — what is eternal cannot be put into relative knowledge nor can it be known by casual interest.

But there are people who have realized the truth and who know the eternal. Whatever they do, whatever they say, becomes an enriching factor to all humanity. The words of Jesus are still here, are they not? The words of Moses still apply. They are real. They cannot depart because their words are of eternal value and are a blessing upon the planet.

You and I can come to eternal truths as well.

But it requires wisdom to receive what is eternal. Although it would be communicated through words, one must go beyond the words to come to the actuality. When we are unable to go beyond the words, we only know what is eternal in an abstract way and thus deprive ourselves of the truth. The word is never the state.

Why do we stop at the level of abstract words? If we remain pacified with words, we stay with the prejudice and limitation of ideas.

If what is being communicated is eternal, then it is accessible to everyone. The idea must be dissolved to come to the actuality. This is a Law. Without this energy to go beyond the words, we stop short. Ideas prevail and we adore them, but ideas separate man from man.

From childhood, the conscious mind is trained and developed. And all through life it is satisfied with ideas. We have to know this in order to overcome the prejudices and knowings that limit us.

A simple question like, "How did *A Course In Miracles* come into being?" opens up a new perspective. The question itself has to be dissolved and brought to the eternal level that is beyond the words, where you receive the stillness, the completeness, the perfection that thought cannot touch. The question can only point the way.

How superior are silence and humility! Humility brings one to an original state of innocence. God would teach you. He protected the innocence when you were a child. He will caress you now and you will feel it. What a curse is this so-called knowing; yet what a heavenly grace is innocence. It is those moments, those split seconds of innocence, that bring the stillness for in those moments He is needed. One's own innocence calls upon Him and His Presence is felt.

The words are not as important as what is not of words because what is not of words extends, and brings one to stillness.

So, we come back to the question, "How did *A Course In Miracles* come into being?"

A Course In Miracles is the Thoughts of God. Someone had to be here, at the physical level, to receive the Thoughts of God. This person would have had to bring herself or himself to complete innocence, free of the externals, in order to be still to receive the Thoughts of God. That also is a Law.

This person would have had to survive all the conditioning of the schools, parents and culture because only in innocence would one know something that is not of this world. Innocence is free from the externals. It is content. It has the capacity to receive. It can come to a stillness, independent of prejudices, likes and dislikes. How amazing it is that this person went through all the drills, yet still retained the purity intact without becoming externalized. Such is the being who is responsible for *A Course In Miracles*.

A Course In Miracles is a gift of God to all mankind. It knows how conditioned and fragmented the human brain has become, and therefore, it brings an eternal action upon that which is of time.

Time does not exist at the level of innocence. Time exists when we cannot cope with an issue, or meet a challenge instantly and directly. Very few people can respond adequately to a challenge. We tend to *react* to anything new that is presented. Thus, time postpones. It can be said that time is an invention of man's inadequacy to meet a challenge.

The Thought of God, however, is not subject to time. It has urgency and tremendous vitality because it does not want to stay in the deception of relative knowledge. It cannot be put into personality for it is boundless.

There is no name on *A Course In Miracles* because it was not brought by personality. A being came who rose to the state of God Consciousness and received the gift to offer to humanity for all times.

Similarly, we see that Mary gave to the world Jesus, the Son of God. She had such purity that when the Archangel Gabriel said to her, "You are to be with a child," these are the words she used,

"Behold the handmaiden of the Lord;
be it unto me according to thy word."[7]

Such a being is rare indeed. Her consciousness, her state, was one that had no reaction in it, no fear in it.

In the ancient sculptures and cathedrals, we see Mary holding the baby not towards herself, but giving the Child to the world. And today, it is as though birth has been given not to Jesus the Child, but to Jesus, the Spirit. And this is what *A Course In Miracles* is. It is not earth-born. It is Christ Consciousness upon the planet.

If you want to bring the Course to application, know that you have His Divine Presence with you. Knowing that He is with you inspires a quality of love and reverence. How would you then sit in His Presence?

Having that kind of reverence, you would see that He is the Teacher. The Unasked Presence would be there. That is why it is so important to know that you are not to *read* the Course, but *live* it. And it is made possible by that Holy Presence. If you read the Course correctly, you would see that He is with you even now.

A Course In Miracles is really holding one by the hand and leading one to living the truths it imparts. So, you have Him as a Teacher.

> *"I go before you because I am beyond the ego. Reach, therefore, for my hand because you want to transcend the ego. My strength will never be wanting, and if you choose to share it you will do so. I give it willingly and gladly, because I need you as much as you need me."*⁸

As we have said, scriptures are thoughts of a purer energy — Thoughts of God. They are the accounts written of those who came and lived amongst us, who were not of this world. Each culture produced its own great beings. We hear the words of sages, prophets, and saints. They are eternal words because they are not timebound. The words of Moses are true whether you are Jewish or not. The words of Guru Nanak are true whether you are Indian or not. The words of Lao Tsu are true whether you are Chinese or not. They do not talk about fragmentation and differences. They have the right to speak of truth because when they speak, it is the Thought of God. Their words are God-lit. And even though they are amongst us on earth, they are of the Kingdom. The values are very different.

The scriptures of the world are holy and they give expression to what is Divine. They point out that you are more than the body and that there is the One God. But since we have heard this in different languages and through various cultures, man's tendency has been to think, "My God is better than your God." Thus, prejudice and friction and religious wars have ensued. Beliefs are earthborn and any belief that fragments is not religious. For then you are limited by your own interpretations and not uplifted by the truth the scripture is imparting.

Everything at the time level degenerates. We see the scriptures of the world have been translated and interpreted. Now one does not even know what is authentic and what is not. Just give it a few centuries and you will see what will happen to *A Course In Miracles*. That is the action of time. That is a Law.

So, the scriptures of the world have gone through translations and there is also the fact that they were written by other people. Moses never wrote, and Jesus never wrote; Buddha never wrote. It was the apostles or those who were nearby who wrote. Some are first person accounts, some verbatim, and some were written down much later. It is extremely important that we understand this because time affects everything on the planet.

But the eternal is never affected. Constantly, other energies, new expressions come into being. And since they are not timebound, they affect.

It became necessary and appropriate then for something like *A Course In Miracles* to appear. Why? First, it has a curriculum of its own. Secondly, it deals with the misperceptions that have crept into Christianity and puts things into right perspective.

This is made very clear in the *Text*:

> *If the Apostles had not felt guilty, they never could have quoted me as saying, "I come not to bring peace but the sword." This is clearly the opposite of everything I taught. Nor could they have described my reactions to Judas as they did, if they had really understood me. I could not have said, "Betrayest thou the Son of God with a kiss?" unless I believed in betrayal.[9]*

Are you beginning to see then how *A Course In Miracles* would be the natural thing to come? It would also not make man dependent — on your own you can read the lesson each day. But the lesson is to be lived and not just read. If you make an idea out of it, you have not understood a thing. *A Course In Miracles* is written for you who are reading it.

There is nothing in the world that has the same systematic, day by day awakening. The Course purifies, awakens and dissolves the conditioning, brings about the unlearning, brings you to that innocence that can know what Heaven is and introduces you to your eternal Self.

In *A Course In Miracles*, like all Divine works, there are keys and there are laws. If you read the Course with your heart and give it that purity of space, He would give you the keys and laws directly. It is difficult to imagine that on this planet anything so powerful, so real, so true exists as *A Course In Miracles*.

> *Nothing real can be threatened.*
> *Nothing unreal exists.* [10]

In just two lines, everything is clarified.

If you put your heart into it for one year, He will teach you. If you are going to have a dialogue with Him, then you will have to put the Course in the first place. Your whole relationship, approach, attitude towards it has to change.

If you put the Course in the second place, and your job and the preoccupation of daily activities in the first place, it will not work. The Course is a way of life and your lifestyle has to change to make the space.

Activity is personal. It is devoid of action. Action is of Life. If the interest is in the Action of

Life and to end the separation, then you would welcome the outgrowing of the unessentials and develop a sense of discrimination. When a man learns the difference between the false and the non-false, that man has come to wisdom and new potentials have awakened within him.

And I know of nothing in the world that can do that better than *A Course In Miracles.*

CHAPTER 3

A COURSE IN MIRACLES
A Need For Reverence

I T IS DIFFICULT to speak of something for which you have the utmost reverence. Reverence is in proportion to your own discovery of the Divinity within.

In relationship with the God-created world,* we have to come to reverence. Because the very glory and holiness of it inspires one. If you were to look at a rose and you really saw what it *is*, it would silence you and bring you to reverence. It has attained its perfection in fragrance and beauty. It is the adoration of the earth for its Creator.

Could you see the perfection of the rose and be

---

*God, the Absolute, created the Son. There is no gap between the Son and the Father. The Son has the energy of the Absolute with which He can create anything He wants, as long as He creates with the same eternal principles with which He was created.

Even though the world was created by the Son, He created it with the energy of the Absolute. The world, then, can be said to be an extension of the Absolute although God Himself, so to speak, is not directly related to its creation.

That which extends is called Creative Energy. It can manifest itself as planets out of which other things evolve: plants, animals, silenced by it? Could you smell its perfume and be so inspired that it awakens other energies in you?

But when you don't have the reverence, you just cut the flower and use it. For a moment you may think it is beautiful. But you never acquaint yourself with those moments of timelessness in which you could outgrow all that is physical. We don't have the space to give so that the rose can flower within us.

Somehow we seem to have lost reverence for all life. Without reverence there is no sensitivity, there is but attachment and possessiveness. The God-created world cannot be bought. Twilight is for those who have reverence and who can afford the great gift of simplicity in which there is the space. What could it do to a person? At twilight, when shadows disappear all becomes One. Duality ends. Would you not have reverence for twilight if it ended your duality?

So to talk about *A Course In Miracles* brings one to humility. One does not dare just talk *about* it. *A Course In Miracles* requires reverence, for its words silence the mind.

What is the origin of words? Words only came into being when man separated from God. There-

---

even the human being and the human brain. All that is part of evolution is of relative existence, subject to measurement and comparison. Thus, the world of opposites comes into being: this is tall, that is short; this is far, that is near; and so forth.

Man, at the level of evolution, projects time. He knows it is now snowing and that there will be another season called spring. Time becomes the basis of his experience, although in reality time does not exist because it is projected. The world of illusion is the projected world made by man.

fore, words can never know reality because they are not real. The origin of words is the origin of separation from that which is eternal.

All our judgments, accusations, and condemnations have no meaning whatsoever. They are a mere play of words.

There was a time when few men knew to read and write. Now most people are educated. But are we any wiser? Are our problems any less? Is insecurity gone? Loneliness is still here and the obsession with "me and mine" increases.

We are not saying that you should be uneducated, only that education does not relate one to Reality. It does not bring one to silence. Knowledge in separation does not bring one to the purity of energy that is ever in harmony. Rather, it brings one to the energy of friction. To be educated, from the Divine perspective, is to be free, independent, liberated, and therefore, an extension of God.

So, what does a mystic or a great being do? He may not be educated, but somehow a veil has been lifted. He is awakened to what is real. His awareness is greater and more spacious than the whole of creation. Not limited to physicality, he is of the Spirit. He encompasses all humanity in his range. He has reverence for every moth and every leaf of a tree. And he gives thanks, like the rose gives thanks, to the earth that provides all things. His mind is still and he is filled with the joy and happiness within that he is part of it all. He begins to see perfection rather than inadequacies in others as well as in himself. He relates with the reality of the human being rather than with his idiosyncracies. He does not condemn his brother for the appetites of his personality. He introduces him to the beauty of his own being.

This is exactly what *A Course In Miracles* does: Introduces each one of us to the impeccable being that we are. Can you imagine anything more sacred than being inspired to your own timelessness?

Anything that has this potential deserves reverence. Because only in reverence is one totally relaxed and able to heed.

All through the New Testament, you see Jesus time and time again, saying: "If you could only hear. If you would please listen. Those who have the ears to hear. . . ."[11]

Since I touched upon *A Course In Miracles* it has become more precious to me than my own life, because without it I did not have a meaningful existence. Therefore, I have reverence for it. For me, it is the Thoughts of God and it lifts me.

To have a relationship with what is true and holy demands purity of self. This you do not need to be taught. You are already it. You are made in the image of God and that impeccable space within you has been guarded forever so that you may get to know yourself.

No one needs to teach you reverence because that is what you are — a Child of God, an expression of eternity on this timebound planet. Such is your holiness. To read *A Course In Miracles* is to be in this Presence and to go beyond the teaching. It brings you to your own sacred Reality and does not make you dependent. Something is given — a blessing of Heaven — whereby you can learn of your own holiness. But the Course requires reverence which has the space and tenderness within to approach it without haste.

Scriptures read with reverence invoke other energies within you. And the gaps between the thoughts begin to widen. This gap is the intensity of your own silence. If scriptures are read unlovingly and hurriedly, this does not take place. Then you only know the words, never your own holiness or your own sacredness.

The purpose of scripture is to end man's duality and separation and bring him to the wholeness that he is. Scripture is only scripture when it is not born out of separation from God. All scriptures are of vertical words and say the same thing: "Love ye one another,"[12] "Know thyself."

A Course In Miracles brings something yet different. Its purpose is to provide self-sufficiency. Reading the lesson invokes within you energies that you have never been sensitive to before. Therefore the important thing is to really learn to read with reverence and space.

Also, the peace within you brings some other vibration wherever you are. It evolves an atmosphere of its own that is never threatened. It knows no insecurity, no unfulfillment, no hate, fear, like or dislike. It is totally independent of all that is made of thought.

In this age, there is the vitality to come to disillusion and to discover the Divinity within that no longer relies upon the externals.

This is how sacred *A Course In Miracles* is, and this is the kind of reverence that is required for you to get acquainted with what it is. Inherent in every line of the Course is the energy to bring you to the truth of it.

When you are in that state, you are not regulated by the externals — outside thoughts and influences. You relate with the externals with wisdom because you are no longer deceived by yourself or by anyone else. Wisdom has its own rightness. Responsible and creative, you add to the harmony of the world. Your rightness directs the action.

This is what *A Course In Miracles* has to impart. Could you not then have reverence for it?

CHAPTER 4

Reading
A COURSE IN MIRACLES

A COURSE IN MIRACLES is a set of books that represent the Thoughts of God. They are not mortal thoughts. If you understood but one sentence of the Course, it would revolutionize your life. Understanding is only understanding when it has brought you to the eternity of God-Thought. And as long as we remain satisfied with the words, without knowing the actuality behind the words, we will never get to know what *A Course In Miracles* is saying.

You cannot read *A Course In Miracles* as long as you are caught in *ideas* because the Course relates to the Actuality of the State. Its words are uttered from that Actuality and its purpose is to bring you and I to its State. Therefore, the man of God would have to be a man of still mind who has seen through all his deceptions. The still mind discovers that he can never learn, that his learning is but a mania for self-improvement, that the brain is ever seeking and perpetuates its preoccupations. This mania of more-ness is what regulates our life. Whether it be for money or for knowledge, we have become victims of this accumulation process.

Man is already perfect but thinks he is not. The realization that all his learning is an indulgence to which he has become addicted brings him to silence. He has touched upon a truth, a discovery within himself. A moment of "KNOW THYSELF" has taken place, and that moment is eternal.

The mind that has freed itself from all illusions and deceptions comes to stillness. It then discovers that any words it utters that are of ideas have no meaning. They are false. For what is an idea based on? . . . "More-ness." Any person who is regulated by ideas — and most of us are — remains unstable and unfulfilled.

Truth is something totally different. Truth is uttered by a state of being. It is part of another energy, the pure energy of Creation, not contaminated by knowings. Nothing of duality touches it. It is neither physical, nor of thought.

Now we can see that even though there are thousands of universities and a great deal of education all over the world, what is called education is merely the training of physical senses in order to survive. And the more we train the senses, the more the defiance of that which is One and the Source. It is a rejection of That, and therefore, man remains a citizen of the earth. This is the statement of separation. And the pain of it reminds us constantly that something is wrong.

The planet itself is tired, worn out. We have burned our nervous energy with more wantings and ideas. We have affluence. And its consequences. Clashes, frictions, duality, conflict, frustrations — on and on.

Peace is of some other purity which is independent of ideas. Peace comes unasked. It is not something you wish and want, for wishing and wanting are of thought. When you come to relaxation, you will discover that peace was always there but you were absent.

So, could you approach *A Course In Miracles* in this manner? First, to come to peace within. Give the daily lesson the space and you will see what it will do. It will activate the Higher Forces within you.

As long as we are caught in ideas we are merely dissipating our energies. Constantly we are fitting things into our own habit patterns, our own scheme of existence, our own schedule. And as long as we remain what we are, it will be difficult to change.

Change is essential because learning is incomplete. Application is necessary.

We cannot merely read the Course. It has to be lived. The Process of Atonement — that which ends the separation — provides the help. It ends duality if we are totally sincere with it. If we are merely reading it as ideas, we are preventing the change from taking place within us.

The real issue is the difficulty of change. Why?

Because we are bound hand and foot to concepts and ideas, to helplessness and to our own belief systems.

But the daily lesson of *A Course In Miracles* has its own vibration and benediction that imparts the energy to bring us to the application of its truth.

Unfortunately, most of us do not know how to read. We read the words but we never touch upon the truth. We are too busy reading. Our reading is thus a brain activity.

We must see that there is the brain and there is the mind. The mind is of God and the brain is physical. So, with the brain, we are attempting to read the words of the Mind of God. But to understand the Thoughts of God, we have to be free of the brain. Otherwise, the brain, being timebound, is also interpreting the words of God and corrupting them while it reads.

Divine Forces have brought us to *A Course In Miracles.* And the Course stresses that God is constantly in communication. But we do not hear.

> *The part of your mind in which truth abides is in constant communication with God, whether you are aware of it or not. It is the other part of your mind that functions in the world and obeys the world's laws. It is this part that is constantly distracted, disorganized and highly uncertain.* [13]

> *Communication . . . remains unlimited for all eternity. And God Himself speaks to His Son, as His Son speaks to Him. . . . How far away*

*from this are you who stay bound to this
world. And yet how near are you, when you
exchange it for the world you want.*[14]

The Course comes to remind us of this contact.
Why is it that we do not heed? Is it that we are not
interested in making the contact with the Holy
Spirit? Do we not want to walk hand in hand with
the Christ whom we meet in the lessons of the
Course? And what is the action of heeding? Is it
possible to end the illusion of separation? Why do
we postpone?

In half an hour, the lesson can dissolve all these
questions. It can also dissolve them within the
minute — if we do not resort to the brain. We have
made of the physical brain our god, but it can never
know the Unknown.

When we listen only through the faculties of the
physical senses — with the brain — we are not
heeding or communicating. The Voice of God is
within each one; yet we cannot hear It because we
are so preoccupied with our brain activity. Thus are
we doomed to the past and to physicality.

If we were to become wise, we would see that
when man separated, "you and me" came into being. This separation created the greed, unfulfillment and suspicion that destroy life. However,
there is still intact within each one an attentiveness,
an awareness as vast as creation, where we are not
separated from God. This is the remembrance we
are trying to invoke.

This is the action of *A Course In Miracles*. Has
there ever been anything more holy or more

sacred? Then why is it that we are not giving it the attention?

What is attention? Attention is not intruded upon by thought. Therefore, it flowers into awareness. Awareness is impersonal and has learned to let go of survival, fear and the accumulative process. Everything else merely increases the separation.

A Course In Miracles brings one to a point of decision. For one has realized that partial attention merely delays and that is all we have known.

The Course stresses that we have to make a decision to put away all partial interests which postpone action. If we do not, further reading of the Course has very little purpose.

> . . . *you need not believe the ideas, you need not accept them, and you need not even welcome them . . . whatever your reactions to the ideas may be, use them. Nothing more than that is required.*[15]

Do you realize what this means? It is saying: THE GRACE OF GOD IS WITH YOU. And every lesson contains this Grace. It will help you. Each person reading a lesson can dissolve the separateness, the physicality, the identity with the ego.

But if, while reading the Course, we are activating the brain, we are also stimulating the memory process. What preoccupies our mind while we are reading the lesson? The past and the future, is it not? If we were dedicated to the Course, would we not make changes in our life?

The Course demands that a change take place with every lesson. As long as there is a resistance to change, we will hold on to "me and mine." The brain has great intelligence for these things. This is its function. It will never let go of its unfulfillment and will always remain unsatisfied. This is its nature. It reads the lesson; but because it is not free, it merely agrees with it and does not change.

The brain does not heed, it agrees. By merely agreeing, we continue to maintain the illusion of "you and me," and are therefore solidifying the separation. And all the knowledge that we receive merely reinforces our earthiness.

We must come to an attentiveness that can heed. When one heeds is where there is wholeness. Attention makes us independent of physicality because it introduces us to a vaster awareness. It is this quality of attention that is needed.

The quality of attention would also see our own tendencies towards laziness and fatigue. It would immediately take steps to ensure that we rest and not dissipate the energy. There is rightness in presenting oneself at the altar of God in the best of health, well-rested, restored. When we have love for the Course this other intelligence comes into being.

We must learn to step out of the momentum of tension and activity and make some space in our lives. We can start simply at first by putting aside time to relax. Without relaxation, it will be difficult to end the projections of the brain.

It takes integrity and courage, wisdom and strength to give honesty to being with what is real. Can we put all our projections aside for one hour? We need to be kind to ourselves. If we fall asleep while reading the lesson, then sleep. We need not go for the "more-ness" of meditation. One day of stillness would change our life. So, give yourself the benediction of relaxation and rest.

Out of that stillness, not pressured by time, we read *A Course In Miracles*. In that relatively still state, where we have the space and are unhurried, we read the lesson and harness the energy of the truth behind the words. The reality of it intensifies the stillness and awakens other Divine faculties. The awakening no longer wants to learn. It is too sweet, too energetic of itself. It blesses even the physical body and brings it to serenity and to the purity of silence.

Unless we awaken to this real gladness within, we will keep on searching, wanting and longing externally. That which is found within is independent of ideas. Ideas themselves are external to who we are.

From this state of silence, whatever we do becomes an expression of the goodness of the Divine Forces that are given to us. Having discovered these Forces are not separate from us, we have the space not to conclude about other people — because the minute we do, we have judged and again fallen into the trap of our knowings. Seeing what others *are* in reality, we could no longer judge them because they hold different ideas or opinions than we do.

A Course In Miracles is for those who can say: "I have come to receive . . ." that which is not of time and evolution, that which is of God. *A Course In Miracles* is the Thought of God each person can receive because each person is related to the Source.

There are a few things that we can begin to do: start the day in a gentle, loving way; awaken earlier, sit quietly; give yourself the space. Do not get busy with errands. They are unending. Be loving to yourself. Do not put yourself in the second place. Rest well. Get up slowly in the morning and be at peace with yourself. Give thanks for a new beginning and read the lesson.

You are going to be speaking with the Father. How would you address Him? Half-heartedly? Partially? Absently? We will have communication when we speak to the Father from our heart, with reverence.

When one is with the present, one becomes interested in the lesson and there is no pressure. If there is the rush to read the Course, then we are doing a duty while we hold in the brain other things that we think we have to do. They become important and not the lesson. We have to discover whether or not we are just doing the lesson as a sense of duty while it is the other things that are in one's heart. The lesson remains incomplete unless one has put love and caring attention into it.

To me, the lesson is like caresses of angels and the fragrance of heaven. It is gentle and pure — a gift of God to His Son. As a Child of God, one is

COMMENTARIES ON A COURSE IN MIRACLES

surrounded by affection. One's heart is full of gratefulness; one enters the world of God.

Would you not read the lesson with that kind of tenderness in your heart? Timelessness brings peace and stillness to the brain when you create a holy atmosphere within yourself.

Make space in your life where there is no intrusion. Read the lesson so that you can communicate with the eternal. And the Course will be your communication with the Light.

Read the lesson in the morning and the *Text* in the evening. The depth of every line goes beyond understanding, to the actual state of recognition where you are no longer separate.

A Course In Miracles has this to impart if you are attentive. This is the gift of the Thoughts of God. This is the gift of *A Course In Miracles*.

> *You are one Self, united and secure in light and joy and peace. You are God's Son, one Self, with one Creator and one goal; to bring awareness of this oneness to all minds, that true creation may extend the Allness and the Unity of God. You are one Self, complete and healed and whole, with power to lift the veil of darkness from the world, and let the light in you come through to teach the world the truth about yourself.*
>
> *You are one Self, in perfect harmony with all there is, and all that there will be. You are one Self, the holy Son of God, united with your brothers in that Self; united with your Father*

in His Will. Feel this one Self in you, and let It shine away all your illusions and your doubts. This is your Self, the Son of God Himself, sinless as Its Creator, with His strength within you and His Love forever yours. You are one Self, and it is given you to feel this Self within you, and to cast all your illusions out of the one Mind that is this Self, the holy truth in you.[16]

CHAPTER 5

The Daily Lesson Is
Your Daily Bread Of Truth

WHAT CONSTITUTES peace? Obviously, its action would be independent of our personality. It would be an action of Creation — the creative action of Life. The birds in flight manifest it. The waves of the sea, the movement of the planets are an extension of the same creative force.

There is a lesson in *A Course In Miracles* which says, *I could see peace instead of this*.[17] What does this mean? It means that the possibility exists to see reality rather than what our thought is projecting; that even though what we see is perceived through thought, there is another seeing altogether that is beyond thought.

Therefore, if you realized *I could see peace instead of this*, then some transformation must take place. You are a different being. You grow in reverence. You grow in humility. You grow freer from the ego. You have more space to give and therefore more space to receive. That is the change that occurs. When we do not allow this to take place, we stop short of peace and make of the lesson a learning. It remains but words. And the word is never the state, never the actuality!

Peace cannot be touched by words or by thought for it is not of personality. This would have to be. The personality is timebound and cannot know the actuality of peace. It knows peace as an idea and *wants* it while it prepares for war.

In order to know peace, there has to be righteousness in life. Yet falsehood is seated on the throne everywhere in the world. Anyone who is somewhat aware and alert must see the degeneration that is taking place. Things are out of control.

In the face of this predicament, the gift of *A Course In Miracles* comes into our hands and says you have to find the peace within yourself. The externals cannot do it. Know that you could have peace instead of this external torment of a world of unreality.

> *Peace of mind is clearly an internal matter. It must begin with your own thoughts, and then extend outward. It is from your peace of mind that a peaceful perception of the world arises.*[18]

We live a life of such stimulation, with no pause to step out of the momentum to hold hands with God. We place our trust in insecurity and not in God. But the Prince of Peace offers His Hand and says:

> *If it helps you, think of me holding your hand and leading you.*

And I assure you
this will be no idle fantasy.[19]

When you hold hands with Him, you step out of time and into eternity. You begin to see that the purpose of time is to bring involvements to an end, that you return to time only to complete your obligations. This is responsibility. This is the right use of time.

Because we exist in relationship, we must not do anything inconsistent with the laws of harmony. When you hold hands with Him, the action of Creation, which is ever perfect, helps you to end your involvements and obligations in a responsible way. There is goodness and kindness in your life for you have brought about a transformation that is related to everyone else.

> *Let Him, therefore, be the only Guide that you*
> *would follow to salvation. He knows the way,*
> *and leads you gladly on it. With Him you will*
> *not fail to learn that what God wills for you is*
> *your will. Without His guidance you will think*
> *you know alone, and will decide against your*
> *peace as surely as you decided that salvation*
> *lay in you alone. Salvation is of Him to Whom*
> *God gave it for you. He has not forgotten it.*
> *Forget Him not and He will make every deci-*
> *sion for you, for your salvation and the peace of*
> *God in you.*[20]

In peace there are no alternatives. It is complete and whole, a gift of God to His Son. All else is secondary — an illusion of which you cannot become a part. You have trust in the Divine Order of Existence.

43

Our interest, however, is not in bringing the self to an end. We trust in manmade ideas and continue the preoccupation of "me and mine." We are not interested in coming to the miracle that ends the past, that brings us to the peace, timelessness and truth of our being.

What is our approach to reading *A Course In Miracles?* Half measures? A duty, ritual, repetition? Can we name one thing we do in which we are totally present?

Let us say there are two approaches. One approach continues the old, the "me and mine," the past. It is the approach of personality with its activity, for the most part, of self-survival and pursuit of safety, security and pleasure. It engenders fear, selfishness, self-centeredness — the illusions of separation. The other approach brings one to newness. It is akin to prayer.

Prayer is not of words; it is the intent within one that is the prayer. It is an action that precedes thought. A prayer that originates in thought is not a prayer. It is a ritual.

A Course In Miracles is meant to end the approach of half measures. But it demands wholeheartedness. To wholeheartedness is given the glory of the lesson. It alone receives the peace the lesson imparts.

Peace liberates man from his own bondage. Bondage can never be improved — not by political systems, not by economic systems, or by organized religions.

We have known only partial action in our life. And now we are given the Thoughts of God offered by *A Course In Miracles* to introduce us to the timelessness of our identity. We are an extension of God here to love one another. We are an extension of the One Life.

To see peace instead of separation, we need to change our approach. We need to come to reverence and total attention to read the Course. The gift you would receive from *A Course In Miracles* would be one that is already yours. You would be most grateful to know that it has always been there but you have been absent.

> *Be confident that you have never lost your Identity and the extensions which maintain It in wholeness and peace.*[21]

A wholehearted approach is innocent of the partial and awakens us to our true identity. Whatever it does, it is an extension of rightness.

The integrity and conviction of rightness can never be affected by the external. Atom bombs, economic depressions, unemployment, recessions — nothing can touch a person who is with rightness.

A Course In Miracles is given to man at a time when he has become dependent on the externals. The Course offers the opportunity to turn from the external to an internal action of God within us.

I could see peace instead of this.

What we see is worry and anxiety at the cost of not seeing peace. Anxiety is manufactured by thought; it is not of God. Love is of God, but we have resorted to hate and fear and war. Society is on a destructive course, but there is hope in the individual. It takes but one man to affect everything in creation. When you have the peace within, the very atmosphere of the planet is blessed.

A Course In Miracles imparts the peace it speaks of. At peace, you are endangered by nothing external. And in this feverish world of panic, fear and pressure, what could be more needed? Could man turn to armament if he were at peace?

We have not yet known the power and the glory of peace. It brings simplicity to life and uproots all that is unessential. Everything is blessed by the Peace of God, by the peace of man. All the resources of heaven and the universe are his because he has learned to receive the peace to give. He has discovered there is no other sharing in the world but the sharing of love. Nothing can touch it. Nothing can frighten it. Nothing can buy it.

When a man has love to give, he is of heaven.

Part 2

The Christ Thought

Hold to the Thought the Christ has placed in you.
This was the Thought which came with you, and gives
Your coming all the purpose that it has.
You have no function but to find this Thought,
To recognize it and to see it as
Your chosen wish, while wishes still prevail,
And the reflection of the Will of God,
Which also is your will. Till that is known,
Accept Christ's Thought, and let it be your own.[1]

CHAPTER 6

A COURSE IN MIRACLES
A New Way Of Life

READING *A Course In Miracles* invokes within the student energies that he may not have been sensitive to before. Its purpose is to provide self-sufficiency and thus, it eliminates the false premise of helplessness.

> *Do you not see that all your misery comes from the strange belief that you are powerless?*[2]

We cannot, however, apply the Course as long as we are satisfied with ideas because *A Course In Miracles* is not an idea. It is not abstract. It does not talk *about* something. It speaks from the actuality of Truth itself rather than from thought.

Only reverence gives us the space to receive that which is not of thought and brings the mind to stillness. Therefore, the important thing is to learn to read with reverence. The very benediction the Course imparts silences one. It is an action of the Grace of God.

Read it lovingly, unhurriedly. The moment you

are relaxed, wisdom will surround you and the Given will become accessible.

A Course In Miracles is the miracle that undoes the belief system of separation.

> *Separation is only the decision*
> *not to know yourself.*[3]

The basic issue we face is the separation in us that promotes fear, loneliness and insecurity, and then, in turn, the wishes and wantings of unfulfillment. Miracles offer us the clarity of inner awakening that is the direct experience of:

> *Nothing real can be threatened.*
> *Nothing unreal exists.*[4]

The miracles of the Holy Instant would bring you to objectivity and reveal this fact.

The Course is a different kind of learning. Man's thought system promotes separation, no matter how sensitive and wise and good its ideas seem. Miracles undo it for they free one from the past and the future. Miracles offer the clarity that frees one from desires, suffering and anxiety which are self-made in ignorance of Reality.

Reality is the Will of God, the Light of perfection. The wise, having seen the fallacy of personal choice, makes but one decision: to never act independent of the Will of God. Thus, he discovers all needs are blessed and met.

REALITY IS THE ONLY DECISION.

Man is meant to be at peace and in harmony with Life, for AS IS is the perfection.

We are talking about *A Course In Miracles* and how to learn from it directly. We need to give it space and read it with a quiet mind that is not pressured. Offer it your stillness and it will be filled with peace. This is a key to studying the Course.

How we approach learning from *A Course In Miracles* and the quality of honesty we give it are all important, for we do not want to turn the teachings of the Course into another belief system within the thought system of man. *A Course In Miracles* is the Thoughts of God and awakens one out of thought to one's own boundlessness.

The Course starts out by undoing our manmade thought system. Undoing is essential because we are so highly conditioned. What we think we know is but our opinion. We stop short, conclude, and therefore, never see the whole, the total.

The Course makes us aware of the false. Whatever questions the manmade thought system is already the new action of God's Grace. It is our conclusions that are being questioned, and the question has the vitality not to accept verbal answers. From the very outset, the Course imparts the energy and clarity to see differently.

> I am *responsible for what I see.*
> *I choose the feelings I experience,*
> *and I decide upon the goal I would achieve.*
> *And everything that seems to happen to me*
> *I ask for, and receive as I have asked.*[5]

The action of *A Course In Miracles* is the action of Love. It does not influence, it awakens. Love is

independent and it must therefore provide freedom and liberation. It restores your identity with
your reality and eternity. One is cleansed with the
purity of:

I am not a body. I am free.
For I am still as God created me.[6]

Where there is the body, there is thought. They
are not two phenomena. If one came to the truth
of, *I am not a body*, then one would say, *I am free*,
and ultimately realize, *I am still as God created me*.
Concepts of punishment, karma and guilt come to
an end.

Within that moment you can behold eternity.
Therefore, you are free from time and discover
your own reality, the sacred moment of your own
boundlessness. This is the moment when the miracle
has taken place. This is the moment in which you
are not a body.

The Course has more to impart than mere intellectual knowledge. Its purpose is to end the separation in one's life and bring one to the wholeness of
one's being. The action of the Course is that instead
of thought, you invite miracles. The miracle is
when time ceases and eternity is. We are talking
about a state where appearances end and the one
Reality is.

Can we approach learning from a new premise
— that of fulfillment? Can we read with an intent to
be free of preoccupation and not to accumulate information? The mania of ''more-ness'' keeps unfulfillment alive and is what regulates our intellectual
faculties. But *A Course In Miracles* is based on each

person's inherent perfection and our approach to reading it should be based on our perfection as well.

If the God we seek is a god born out of unfulfillment, he will end up being a projection of our unfulfillment — an image — and not the Truth. The Course says,

"God is with me. I live and move in Him.[7]

Separated as we are, we tend to separate everything. Anything to which you give a name, that is in isolation, is unreal because everything is part of the whole. Unless we see the whole, we are not seeing at all.

Nothing can function in isolation. True relationship exists at the eternal level in which there is no fear, insecurity or unfulfillment.

When you have seen the limitation and falseness of ideas, you will come to stillness and communicate with something beyond your own thought. This is the purpose of the Course, to bring ideas that cannot know love or truth to an end. The ability to see the false as the false is to be free of the false. That moment of freedom is religious. That is the space where the miracle takes place.

We usually do not listen, we interpret. We interpret what we hear; we interpret what we read. We only listen to our interpretations, and the chatter goes on. The minute you are really attentive, however, thoughts cease.

The thought process is not real. It is of ideas. Ideas, like emotions, are changeable. They subside, rise and fall. There is no consistency in them. Consistency exists in attentiveness because, in that moment, we are free from the activity of the brain. The space to recognize we are part of the Mind of God is provided when the chatter of the brain is silenced and no longer interferes. Then we discover that every single person is blessed being part of the Mind of God, and the separation ends between "you" and "me." At the brain level, there is separation. At the Mind level, we are all One.

It is the Mind of God that is religious and not the brain. The brain can be Christian, Hindu or Moslem, conditioned and shaped as it is by the environment and personal experience. On the other hand, the Mind of God is neither conditioned nor subject to experience.

Each lesson of *A Course In Miracles* brings to our awareness our separation, and offers the miracle to undo it. Once that fact is established, our relationship with the Course changes. We become more attentive and read it differently. Every sentence leads from our thought to the Mind of God. This is the unique gift of the Course.

When we read the Course, there is the questioning of our unrealized words and the discovery of our attachment to our thought — thus, an awakening to the newness beyond the words. This actuality of direct experience takes place if there is the attention.

My mind is preoccupied with past thoughts. [8]

Because most of us are lost in the past, we cannot receive the creative energy of the Present. Lesson after lesson, the Course begins with questioning and undoing to get us out of the past. It says:

I see nothing as it is now.[9]

The Course begins with awakening. It is a course in miracles so that you come to a truth — to a wholeness — and to rightmindedness. It is in rightmindedness that miracles take place.

As we read, we begin to value what *A Course In Miracles* is, and the reverence and love for it increases. As we free ourselves from the manmade world, we see that the God-created world is the sustainer. We observe how we cut ourselves off from the God-created world through our anxieties and worries, how we spend our lives and God-given energy supporting the meaningless.

Within every lesson is the blessing to bring one to the clarity of truth. It is His Will, His Power, His Blessing that its goal be accomplished, within one year, by anyone who studies it with integrity and devotion. Please realize what this statement means. What else could you ever want?

If there is the potential in one lesson to bring us to wholeness, how would you approach it? Casually? Hurriedly? Would you try to fit it into your scheme of life, into your schedule? If so, you are not ready to fit into God's Mind. Are you willing to kindly observe this?

Are you reading *A Course In Miracles* as an idea, to improve yourself? The minute you have reduced it to ideas, it is no different than anything else. And the self continues. Somewhere we have to see that we must outgrow the self.

> *Forget not that the motivation of this course is the attainment and the keeping of the state of peace. Given this state the mind is quiet, and the condition in which God is remembered is attained. . . .*
>
> *To learn this course requires willingness to question every value that you hold. Not one can be kept hidden and obscure but it will jeopardize your learning. No belief is neutral.*[10]

Are you approaching *A Course In Miracles* because you really want to step out of the constant preoccupation of thought that gives you no rest? Do you want to bring the deceptions of the brain to silence? If there is that burning need, then your relationship with the Course becomes different.

Yet people have read it over and over without realizing the truth of it. Can you read it with the intensity of an attentive mind that will bring you to the State? It will require that you place a challenge before yourself. Without seriousness, the reading becomes a ritual. The brain loves habit for it functions in terms of routine. Where does your energy go? How do you dissipate it? It is this questioning that brings about a change in lifestyle.

Each sentence in the Course confronts us with a challenge. Can we give it the inner space to unfold? Usually, when a challenge comes, we put it off. We do not recognize the cause of the inadequacy that cannot respond to a challenge in the moment. Helplessness is but our belief. It is not a reality.

The action of helplessness is compromise. Are you willing to put compromises away — instantly

— as you read? This is application. This is discovery.

The vitality of urgency alone can deal with the nonchalant attitude of compromise and, in so doing, come to passion.

A Course In Miracles is a joyous adventure. The daily lesson carries its blessing all day long. You need never be touched by the fear of insecurity for fear is largely psychological. Thus, you begin to extend the peace of God on earth knowing you are not alone.

We stand together, Christ and I,
in peace and certainty of purpose.[11]

What a benediction to know that you have never been alone! Light and Love, the Given, have always surrounded you. To realize that the Given is accessible is the strength.

The next step is to realize that you and your brother are the extension of One Life. No longer looking upon what he does in the body, you see his holiness. To the Christ-State, the body and thoughts are external, for they are of the world of separation.

The choice is either peace or the thoughts of past and future peopled with personalities and unreality. You want the peace of God, but it cannot be without letting go of the illusion of past and future ordeals.

The words of *A Course In Miracles* inspire one to the state of stillness. They carry its eternal peace and awaken the Light in you.

Please do not underestimate yourself.
You carry the blessing with you.
Be at peace,
and know that you are part of eternity.

> *The certain are perfectly calm,*
> *because they are not in doubt.*
> *They do not raise questions,*
> *because nothing questionable enters their minds.*
> *This holds them in perfect serenity,*
> *because this is what they share,*
> *knowing what they are.*[12]

CHAPTER 7

A COURSE IN MIRACLES
A Response To The Sorrow Of Man

WE GIVE SUCH importance to concepts and ideas. Everything is based on them: wars, likes, dislikes, nationalities — the fragmented world. How man maintains the separation and distorts wholeness is the story of humanity. But can there be truth where there are concepts? Where is the man who is not caught in them?

We have even made truth into a concept: my "truth" versus your "truth." Truth and love and peace are not personal because they are of the Kingdom of Heaven where there is no separation between "you" and "me" — there is only the One which ends all conflict, all concepts and projections. The One is impersonal, personality is not.

Personality cannot know love. It can like things and become attached to someone or something. But love would be moments that are involuntary, as if given. And the Given is to be received for giving and receiving are one action. We have separated the two. Now the Given is no longer truly received.

The Kingdom is always extending its grace, its love, its peace and truth. Yet we are too preoccupied with the "me and mine," the personal, to receive. The personal has become quite a problem. And we do not know how to step out of it because we use thought as the means for doing so, and thought is by nature personal. We have never used love to step out of it because we would then have to end the personal. Listen to this carefully. We have used the *concept* of love; we have used the *concept* of truth. We say, "I am honest." "I love you." "I want truth." But that which is separated, the "I" is always present. Personality is a short term affair and it has imprisoned us. And we want to improve it, which is where the activity begins. But the concept of the separated "I" remains.

It is only the physical eyes that separate us. But if we looked through the eyes of Christ, there would be no separation. (When I talk about Christ, I am not necessarily talking about the man Jesus. Christ is a State of Being; it is the only Son. The Son is a State and not a physicality.) One looks, not with physical eyes, but with the Light of Heaven. Only the Light of the Kingdom sees what is true, that which is peace, that which is love.

We must question our concepts and ideas, our belief systems and dogmas! Confronting illusions is the first step of undoing. You alone can do it. But we are so insecure that in present society, survival has become the issue. Do you realize how conformed we have become in order to survive in this world, to make a living? Everything is owned by the corporations. Commercialized life and education but serve the system. Skills are needed to support the personality — the body — but skills will never relate man to Reality. How highly trained one has to be today to make a living! And the computerized society has just begun. These are but facts.

The person who is religious does not react to it nor does he try to organize a cause against it, for then he would be in the same trap. The religious person is only concerned with deceptions and he begins with himself. He questions: "To what do I give my energy?"

When you are depleted, what do you value most? Outlets. Society today revolves around outlets. Outlets are needed because it is unnatural to be doing something abstract and unessential. Man's life is no longer holy and sacred upon the earth.

Begin to see this everywhere. There is hardly a friend in sight because our words do not last. We have become people of expedience. We can say, "I like you," but circumstances come to change those words. Virtue and truth are forgotten. All that remains is to make a living. This is reducing life to physicality.

But what about the Life of the Spirit? We are not just physical.

The status quo must be seen as it is — and not with cynicism but as a fact. We do not necessarily have to have an opinion about it. To see something for what it is is the way to end interpretations. But the incessant activity of the brain has taken over our life. It cannot come to silence, to the moment of wholeness that is blessed and ever accessible.

As long as man is not whole, he must belong to something. And therein lies the danger. Mankind everywhere is becoming destructive and is moving towards war. Can we witness the consequences of nationalism? If we understood its effects, we could never be nationalistic again. It does not matter whose nationalism it is. Nationalism is a concept of separation that rules our life. Yet, as we have said, concepts and ideas are not real.

To live without knowing what is real is rather sad. We have to dull ourselves in order to do so. We have to desensitize ourselves to lead a life that is false. And yet we try to improve the false life through education. See the paradox. Does the educated person know the truth of *I am as God created me?*[13] If he does not, what good is his education? If it does not lead to truth or to a virtuous life, then what good is his education?

In the absence of knowing our own eternity, we are caught in the pressures of time, circumstances and situations. Therefore, we find no lasting relationships, no friendships, no love. Even the relationship between parents and children has become affected everywhere. And it is getting worse.

Somewhere we have to begin the action within ourselves, for it is the self-actualized human being who will break out of the collective culture. We begin with first discovering: "Why is there lack of peace in my life? Why is it that I am not happy?"

In the absence of happiness, we need the gratification of outlets. Where there is gratification, there is sorrow also. What is this lack of fulfillment in a person? We have substituted pleasure for joy, attachment for love and opinion for truth. Have you met anyone who has gone beyond these substitutes? See the chaos it has brought into the world.

With the increase of prosperity and affluence, the unfulfillment of man has intensified. Man's world revolves around unfulfillment. We have become convinced and conditioned that there is lack in creation. A desire-ridden life is devoid of peace and joy. It seeks pleasure and the gratification of the senses which bind one to physicality. It is the adoration of nothingness through which man perpetuates his torment.

It is time for us to question. To do this we need silence and simplicity. Can we afford to be simple anymore? What are we going to give our children if we have not the wholeness, the simplicity and the wisdom to impart? Without these, they will be subject to the pressures of time and circumstances. Without these man remains blinded by his wantings. The unfulfillment of desire rules him. This sorrow of man compels him to go for pleasure. Having violated all laws of morality, virtue and ethics, bodies are abused and decadence prevails. Pleasure is for sale in proportion to the sorrow in our lives. And it is very costly. These things we have to discover and the potential is in man to do so.

How little we know of our own glory, of our own eternity. Each person is a stranger unto himself. To discover one's own perfection should be of first importance. What would it take to cleanse ourselves of educated ignorance and come to innocence — even for a moment — to be what we really are: impeccable, unconditioned, sinless? If you have made the decision to know love or to know God, it would be given you. Your purity would blossom. It would be a laughter and a joy within you forever. Because whatever a thing is is what it extends; when you are related to what is eternal, you have something to give to the world that it desperately needs.

Never in the history of man has he been so helpless. What power has the individual human being against the escalating arms race? Nations blame each other and justify the accumulation of deadlier weapons. What is virtuous about division? Do you not see the tension it promotes as a result of territorial rights? Is the world seeking protection in love and innocence, or in armament? This is the issue of man upon the planet. The insanity is universal. All society is the same. It is based on fear, advantages and anger. Whenever you become survival-oriented, you give your energy to fear and you are part of the nothingness and unreality of the world.

Fear comes into being when you have nothing to give to the world. But the one who steps out and discovers his own perfection is no longer subject to hate and division. He is part of the wholeness of Life. The challenge is before you to recognize that you are an eternal being. It is time for each person to become responsible for finding the peace within. It is not something to be achieved. It is merely that you are absent from it; thus you are helpless and in the grip of sorrow. Only when you are whole is there the love that would take care of these issues. In truth, no one is isolated.

Man is not limited to physicality and somewhere within him is the cry for something real. In response to this yearning, *A Course In Miracles* has been given to mankind. There are many lessons in the Course that help man to overcome the sorrow of today's world. How do you listen to this lesson beyond the idea and the concept?

I trust my brothers, who are one with me. [14]

If you received this one truth you would be silenced and transformed. Never again would you fit into personality. You would be of the Kingdom of Heaven. Having discovered the right purpose of the body, you bring what is of God to earth and extend love, truth, peace.

How will you silence the brain in order to know what is whole? It matters little whether you are educated or not, whether young or old. The challenge is one and the same. Would you trust everyone? As long as there is attachment and fear, could you afford to do so?

We are caught in the collective consciousness that knows no urgency and lives by partial attention. This we must see. But once you are awakened, you are a gift to all mankind. Nothing can then hide your light. And what you bring will remain upon this planet. Such is the life that is productive according to God's perspective.

And so the lesson reads:

I trust my brothers, who are one with me.

We have twenty-four hours to receive the truth of this, because then another lesson is given. There is no doubt about the truth being given. Why is it that we cannot receive? We do not hear the words of truth because we are listening to our interpretations. Heeding means that we are no longer with thought. Once having heeded, it would change our life.

And we come to the next lesson:

I will be still an instant and go home. [15]

What is home? We have lost relationship with Heaven, with our eternity; we have lost relationship with the one instant of stillness.

The next lesson states:

I call upon God's Name and on my own.

God's Name is holy, but no holier than yours. [16]

We do not think our father is God. And everything becomes limited and small. How the professionals and organized religions have reduced man to littleness. They have been detrimental, rather than introducing him to his perfection.

> *To call upon His Name is but to call upon your own. A father gives his son his name, and thus identifies the son with him.* [17]

The collective mind does not recognize this as helplessness however. And man remains in a delirium. What conformity there is the world over.

His brothers share his name, and thus are they
united in a bond to which they turn for their
identity.[18]

When I see you as a brother, you introduce me
to the Oneness. The brain, on the other hand, introduces me to the separation of ''you'' versus
''me.'' It is only possible to say, ''Love ye one
another''[19] where there is Oneness. Fear could
never touch you then. You will never be uncertain
about what to do because duality will have ended.
Love is not of the earth. And we must not accept
the concept and the idea of love as real.

Repeat the Name of God, and call upon your
Self, Whose Name is His. Repeat His Name,
and all the tiny, nameless things on earth slip
into right perspective. Those who call upon the
Name of God can not mistake the nameless for
the Name, nor sin for grace, nor bodies for the
holy Son of God. And should you join a brother
as you sit with him in silence, and repeat
God's Name along with him within your quiet
mind, you have established there an altar
which reaches to God Himself and to his Son.[20]

The Name of God is that which silences all other
names and introduces you to your state of being, to
the actuality of that eternity. The Name of God is
an action that transforms the individual and brings
him to his reality. It is free of consequences. And if
you read it with that silence, you will know it.

The next lesson continues:

The Name of God is my inheritance.[21]

Reading this, do you not want to jump for joy? What has happened to us that we can no longer be ignited? Just the inspiration of it! That we are like Him! This lesson of *A Course In Miracles* has the potential and the benediction to introduce you to the reality of which it speaks. What more can one ask?

Then the next lesson:

I want the peace of God.[22]

Have you ever wanted the peace of God? Have you ever longed for it and meant it?

I want the peace of God.

To say these words is nothing. But to mean these words is everything. If we could but mean them for just an instant, there would be no further sorrow possible for you in any form; in any place or time. Heaven would be completely given back to full awareness . . .[23]

You and I can invoke those powers within us and come to that awareness. When you say, *I want the peace of God,* it is an invocation that will never be denied. Say this wholeheartedly and know that it will come.

No one who truly seeks the peace of God can fail to find it.[24]

CHAPTER 8

A COURSE IN MIRACLES
And Religion

M AY WE BEGIN by examining the origin of religion as man knows it? Civilization, thus religion, began on a regional basis. People were scattered in different parts of the world, with limited communication between them. Each of these regional groups evolved certain saints, mystics and prophets. Religions centered around these.

Gradually, regional civilization produced art, crafts, singers and dancers. It also produced hatred and fear with its inevitable clashes and great wars. Whenever any mind is fragmented, there is friction.

Manmade ideas and concepts only exist at the time level where there is separation. At the God-level, there is Love. It has no nationality; it is not part of regional civilization. There is no fragmentation in Love. We are children of eternity but the minute we step into manifestation, the problems begin. Problems are only at the thought level.

It takes a great deal of wisdom to discover that thought is always biased. In the absence of wisdom, ideas become the prison of man. We are not talking about opinions and points of view. These are facts. A fact is an observation of what is, and therefore, devoid of opinion. Being a witness, you observe although you remain uninvolved. True observation is only possible where there is the still mind.

The still mind sees that in God's world every moment is perfect. But in the manmade world of projections, there is constant change and friction.

Religion as it exists today is, for the most part, belief. Man is conditioned to believe in something he does not know directly. Hence, he becomes dependent on ideas. This cannot be said to be religious.

In the nineteenth and the twentieth centuries great beings emerged who were not merely prophets or saints — they were Extensions. What then is the difference between a saint, a prophet and an Extension?

A prophet is usually one who organizes religions.

A saint is one who emerges out of religion and outgrows it. If he is a saint, he no longer belongs to any conventional religion. Once man has come to sainthood, he is no longer fragmented. He stands with his head in Heaven because he is no longer representative of man's regional civilization with its concepts and ideas. He maintains that all men are of God and sees all life as One Life. Every religion has the potential to bring one to sainthood if one is wholehearted.

Extensions are those who have never separated

from God. They extend the Will of God and do not form religions.

There is much we can learn about religious life from the Extensions. Rather than to build a following based on dependence, they proclaim that we have the same capacities as they. The Extension does not belong to any concept or idea. He is of a silent mind. He is truly religious who encompasses all humanity in his range.

A Course In Miracles is religious in the truest sense. It consists of no external form of religion or dogma. It does not convert. Rather it introduces you to the reality that you are.

I am the holy Son of God Himself.[25]

A Course In Miracles says that *you* are an Extension. It is one of the greatest gifts of God to man.

Religion begins with "Know thyself." This is the challenge. There is much in us that remains unresolved. We have to question our impurities, our prejudices, our ideas — to dissolve them, not replace them.

To be free of our knowings is to be free from the bondage of beliefs and to come to the purity of silence. If we know not what Love is, all our knowing is meaningless. Only Love knows the holiness of which we are a part. Therefore, it cannot destroy. It cannot let ideas make us hateful. Love is of God; hate is regional and political. It is a belief; it is of survival.

In what way has civilization helped man to overcome insecurity and fear? Has it not added to it? If we saw this, we would be less boastful of our tribal beliefs and nationalisms.

Conventional religion has not freed man from the tribal mind nor from his self. It wants to improve the self. What a contradiction that man would want to improve what God has already created perfect!

Do you not yearn to be free of belief systems and borrowed thoughts, of the bondage of the self and all its sickly knowings? Do you not want to know the State that will never compromise? Unless we come to that State, we will not know God.

Man has difficulty being wholehearted and serious about anything. Thought dominates his brain as long as he limits himself to partial attention which always has duality within it. In partial attention, man becomes casual and tends to follow someone else's beliefs and ideas.

It is religious to question every belief you hold and silence your own thought. You become a Light unto yourself, your own teacher, your own pupil. You can no longer be deceived by another nor by yourself. And you burn to know the truth that liberates man from his thoughts and beliefs. At every step you dissolve the ideas. This is called self-sufficiency. It is a moment of purity within you that thought cannot touch.

With the humility of "I don't know," thought is defeated. Stillness then begins to expand. What does the action of stillness do? It brings all thoughts to silence.

The nature of thought, being of the time level, is

that it continually postpones. And therefore, it cannot be with the living moment. Thought can only function in the illusions of past or future.

The Present is the only Reality. It is the Present that imparts the energy to bring the mind to stillness and introduces us to the truth that we are children of eternity.

The Present is not fragmented. When you are in the Present, what you say is an extension of the totality of Life. And you become the Extension of God, the Extension of the Unknown. Ideas dissolve and you communicate something beyond the thought.

The ability to see the false as the false is to be free of it. That moment of freedom — which no other person can give you — is religious. It is your own silence which awakens you to the Mind of God, of which we are all a part. The question is, are you approaching *A Course In Miracles* because you want to bring your deceptions to an end?

If there is that burning need, then your relationship with the Course becomes reverent. But where lack of seriousness exists, things become a ritual, a routine. These are the facts.

Learn what it is not to compromise.

Religion is a State of Being and remains innocent and silent. It requires understanding why we compromise. Find out whether you really want a religious life that is a State and not a dogma. And know that:

RELIGIOUS LIFE IS NOT DECEIVED.

CHAPTER 9

A COURSE IN MIRACLES
Versus Relative Knowledge

HAVE YOU EVER been so quiet that something in you resists getting down to the brain level to formulate thought? This would be the mark of a silent mind. It is not an imposed silence, but one that has seen that nothing one knows has any meaning. It is a silence which comes after you have done a lot of work in emptying yourself, coming to purity. It is very energetic. But this is an energy you have to earn.

How does one earn that energy should be your question. If we are serious-minded, this is what we would ask. Without wisdom there can be no silence; without discrimination there is no silence; without virtue there is no silence. Silence, then, must be virtuous, wise, discriminate and untouched by desires.

The silent mind sees the fallacy of the accumulated knowledge the human being has stored in his memory for millions of years. It looks at it from a timeless state and *observes* — in a simple way, unhurriedly. This state is not of time. It does not know haste and pressures. It is not interested in learning, so to speak. It sees that education has become horizontal and has lost touch with the vertical. It has become what is known as relative knowledge. Man probably never thought relative knowledge would one day destroy man. But that is nearly its sole purpose now — to kill the human being.

You would have to be still and silent to see this. So still and silent that the thoughts do not come from the brain. So still and silent that the brain itself dare not move. It is so attentive, alert, energetic. Just by observing one's own brain, one begins to understand the growth of relative knowledge and everything that has taken place over the eons.

The individual is the maker of the very environment to which he has become a slave. But he also has the power to break away from it and end its conditioning — to create a new environment that will not dull his mind and spirit.

What do you think relative knowledge is? What are its effects? What a tragedy we have never questioned relative knowledge! Relative knowledge has made us helpless. It cannot outgrow desire. It has no need for wisdom.

Because of our belief in relative knowledge, we get stimulated by the energy of the flag — nationalism, by the energy of the military — defense, and by the energy of money — survival and gratification. These forms of energy we interpret as strength while in actuality they promote weaknesses in us because they rule our lives, determine our moods, our behaviors. All this silence sees.

Relative knowledge is the basis of our education. Today it is compulsory, almost mandatory that you be programmed. It limits you by telling you you are an American, or you are a Chinese. There are linguistic divisions; there are racial divisions. It is all of relative knowledge and makes one more and more limited. Is education no more than the teaching of prejudices? Does a young child know the difference between democracy and communism; what is Islam and what is Hindu?

This mandatory education has imposed a limitation upon man and we have become its slave. We abide by it. Sheer helplessness. Limited to just our own resources, we now need something to take care of us — a machine, a factory, an office, an army.

See the wild animals — the gazelles, the mountain lions — the joy of their life. So alert. Such reflexes. Even the plants and the mushrooms are free to grow. Not the human being. We are like the cattle behind the fence. It is one big poultry farm.

Our affluence and our technology and our dogmas make it almost impossible to know a truth. We can only be a wage-earner with some skill. Can we see this objectively? We are almost totally paralyzed, programmed never to want any wisdom, any truth. We cannot afford it because time costs money according to governments and corporations. Therefore we are bound and regulated by our own ignorance and fear. Has progress awakened in man a yearning for what is eternal? What has happened to man upon the planet! Isolation and fragmentation are stamped upon our destiny!

Having lost innocence, we are now with conflict and everything that is born of conflict has its consequences. Vested interest now rules the nations — it rules politics, it rules the military, it rules commerce, it rules human life. And the human being, with all his relative knowledge, can hardly escape. Hijackings, terrorism, suspicion, fear, oppression — we are controlled people. The only things that matter are beliefs and dogmas and abstract concepts. We are lost in coins and calculations — totally locked in by the brain. Behold the desolate, desecrated altar of our life! Never touched by the Mind of God, it is a violation of holiness.

Spiritual life is the divine wealth of a man before the altar of God.

Father, today I am Your Son again.[26]

We cannot hear this. The Father calls and even though we read it, we do not hear. There is no unity within and no unity without. Silence and innocence unify. Intensity of interest silences the mind. But we remain interested in things of the brain for the most part, things of relative knowledge which are but expressions of unfulfillment.

A Course In Miracles comes offering God's Plan for Salvation. And we bring it down to the level of relative knowledge because that is all we know. We read it but we cannot hear it. It is Absolute Knowledge and we are prisoners — shackled, educated with relative knowledge for things of the earth. Fear is of the earth; desire is of the earth; unfulfillment is of the earth; war and conflict are of the earth. And with these we violate humanism.

What does one do with such conditioning, such lethargy, such physicality, such limitation? What would help? Have you not felt the pain and anguish of this? We have known to pacify ourselves with indulgences and to drug ourselves with an immoral life of gratification — a life of the body senses, nothing else. We need to discover that relative knowledge is the home of insanity. This is what *A Course In Miracles* points out.

God's Plan for Salvation talks about the law of completion. The law of completion means the ending of desire. The ending of desire is the ending of relative knowledge — the ending of limitation and conflict within. Then you can say:

Father, today I am Your Son again.

for you have ended all desire. It is a State of Being that is not subject to the brain.

Consider ''In God We Trust.'' What does it mean? Once you trust in God, you have ended conflict totally. You do not trust the relative anymore. You trust in God and this trust would burn the relative. Take a firm stand so that the relative cannot affect you and move you and induce you and frighten you with its insecurity and unfulfillment.

''In God We Trust'' is the ending of conflict, the

ending of relative knowledge, the ending of unful-fillment. Only then can you say:

I am here only to be truly helpful.
I am here to represent Him Who sent me.
I do not have to worry about what to say
or what to do,
because He Who sent me will direct me.[27]

Are you willing to be directed? Have you any relationship with Him Who is in charge of the process of Atonement?[28] We have to make this change — *if* you can change, want to change. It is up to you.

I TRUST. Then you are already with silence — the energy of totality with its tremendous vitality and vast resources. This is the silence we have been speaking of. A silence so total that it hesitates to enter the realm of thought.

One comes to humility. Humility has a space and quiet about it. It begins to undo the boasted panaceas of relative knowledge and to outgrow it step by step. It questions everything and by questioning, gains momentum and energy. Every time you question, you are releasing the hold relative knowledge has over you and coming closer and closer to the One Who is in charge.

Religious life begins when you can say,

I will not value what is valueless.[29]

With that humility and that conviction, you see the fallacy, the limitation, the madness of a life of rela-tive knowledge. You bring gratefulness to yourself and peace to your sleep, your day, your night.

They become blessed because you are no longer tormented by inner conflict. You have trust.

The key to God's Plan for Salvation is undoing because in the undoing there is insight. Insight is independent of thought. It cleanses the mind of all the past experiences of mankind upon the planet — not just your individual dogmas and prejudices. Everything. It cleanses the very cells in the brain. It undoes and purifies you and brings you to the state of:

My single purpose offers it to me.[30]

Another dignity, another poise. Then you can say, ''Yes.''

Father, today I am Your Son again.

You have insight to dissolve all that is of the earth. You stand as a light upon the planet, a light amongst men. Insight brings the Kingdom of God to earth. And that is the function of *A Course In Miracles* — God's Plan for Salvation.

CHAPTER 10

A COURSE IN MIRACLES
As Absolute Knowledge

THIS IS A COURSE in liberation. The minute you recognize the truth — which takes no effort — a miracle takes place. The minute you identify with fear and separation, you rely on thought, turning your back on that miracle. Which would you have: a miracle or thought?

Absolute Knowledge cannot be deceived by thought. It must come because it is a Law. It will come because this is a course in miracles.

The words of the Course represent Absolute Knowledge not relative knowledge. And for the most part, we do not know what Absolute Knowledge is. What kind of mind would it require to receive that which is Absolute?

In the *Workbook for Students,* the first lesson is:

Nothing I see. . .means anything.[31]

This is Absolute Knowledge. Do you see the truth of it? Nothing we see means anything, but we think it does. Even if we agree with the words of the lesson, it does not mean we have heard them. We are in the bondage of what we know; therefore, we remain ignorant of the Absolute. Each lesson of the Course poses a challenge. And this we avoid.

Beyond greed and fear, wanting and wishing, what do we know? We are limited to a small sphere of existence. It is strictly a self-centered life in which we are preoccupied all day long with nothing more than the activity of the physical brain. Yet Life is more than that.

When the Course says,

> Nothing I see. . .means anything.

and

> I have given everything I see. . .
> all the meaning that it has for me.[32]

what do you hear? When you listen to the truth of it, every word brings the mind to a greater intensity of stillness rather than to reaction, activity or interpretation. You transcend it all. Thus, it is different from mere reading.

Truth, being limitless, has in it the ability to bring one to boundlessness. This limitlessness is the Unknown. It just is. It cannot be learned. But stillness can receive it. Complete unto itself, it is Absolute.

He who heeds is no longer in the bondage of what he knows. He has nothing to defend and nothing to protect, for the activity of the physical senses has ceased and he has come to peace.

What then is the action of Truth? It undoes all

that we know and frees us from our bondage. See that wherever there is attachment or vested interest, we become threatened. The man we like least is the one who brings the gift of truth, for he is a threat to the ego. Where threat exists, there is no interest in the Absolute Knowledge of God. Fear wants to make of God a Hebrew, a Hindu or a Christian. Is it possible? Can fragmentation come from a mind that is whole?

Organized religions have their dogmas, but you are the Son of God. You are not fragmented; you are part of the whole. You are bigger than creation. Limit not yourself to the physical senses, but be the Spirit that you are, and you will find within you a light brighter than a thousand suns. It knows — not verbally or intellectually — the truth of,

I am sustained by the Love of God.[33]

Knowing your holiness, you will never subordinate yourself. You will extend your holiness rather than become part of the relative knowledge which divides man from man; where ideas are important and not truth.

My meaningless thoughts
are showing me a meaningless world.[34]

Are we willing to see that our thoughts are meaningless? Why are we attached to them? We are frightened to let go of what we think. Where there is fear, we hold on to what is manmade and the preoccupation with survival prevents us from knowing what is real. Once we have had a vision of the world God created, we will no longer fit into the world of convention.

See what man has done, century after century, in the name of religion and education, science and progress. Has it not placed man at the mercy of the system?

This is the price we pay for being slaves of relative knowledge. It knows no freedom, only dependence. Because man has lost confidence in himself and in his own holiness, survival has become the force that rules him. It does not matter where one is in the world, the principle is the same.

Relative knowledge has its own belief system because it does not have truth. We are in the bondage of what we believe. And if what you believe is different from what I believe, then there are the clashes. Beyond "me and mine," it is difficult for us to go. "Me and mine" is not interested in Absolute Knowledge. And *A Course In Miracles* is of Absolute Knowledge. Therefore it must, by definition, threaten the relative.

The Course clearly states:

What you project you believe.[35]

What we project is always something we already know. We cannot project the unknown. Therefore, we have to undo the past for this Absolute Knowledge of God can only be received if we are in the Present. Only then are we true to ourselves and free from all our knowings. When the past does not intrude, you are a light unto yourself. This state can be called religious.

We are talking about what will end seeking and learning beyond boundaries and time — where nothing can bind you anymore. That alone is real; that alone is Absolute.

Why then have we gone for partial knowledge? We are responsible for limiting our lives to the conscious mind that knows nothing other than self-survival and pleasure. And so, we needed *A Course In Miracles.* Somewhere one has yearned for it even though the conscious mind does not give us a moment of stillness.

The purpose of the Course is to awaken the deep need within us for what is real so that the conscious mind can heed it and make it a part of our life. When there is no conflict, we have ''. . . the ears to hear''[36] and can share what is Absolute. As long as there is conflict within, we will go on interpreting. Interpretation cannot receive. When we settle for it, have we not denied peace and love and truth?

To limit ourselves to the conscious mind has become rather dangerous for it does not know holiness. We have become destroyers of life upon the planet. Mankind itself is at stake. Irresponsibility can never be comprehended by the conscious mind because it knows no love; it does not care for another. In the end, it does not care for itself either.

We need the timeless to be free of the bondage of time. That is why *A Course In Miracles* has been given. It is timeless and it can free us. Can you imagine that we do not have the space to read it with a quiet mind?

The question remains: How are we, as human beings, going to acknowledge our holiness? This should bring us to urgency because casualness cannot receive what the Course has to give.

You and I are capable of knowing what is eternal directly. It is possible for man to know truth. But one's commitment to knowing truth has to be total. As long as one is preoccupied with interpretations, there is no way for the Absolute to enter. We must discover Absolute Knowledge within ourselves. Relative knowledge has a place, but without its relationship to the Absolute, it is valueless.

Relative knowledge has taken confidence out of man. We trust nothing because we do not have a relationship with the Real. When one is related to that which does not change, one has confidence.

A Course In Miracles is the Voice of Absolute Knowledge. It says:

> *Nothing real can be threatened.*
> *Nothing unreal exists.*[37]

You cannot debate about it. And as a fact, it begins to undo what is of relative knowledge: prejudices, belief systems, dogmas. This done, you come to a wholeness in which you know directly — not the word — but the actuality of it.

The planet needs such a being who is related to his eternity. Each person becomes like a holy tree of light upon the earth. And the fruit of your life is the holiness you impart to others.

Part 3

Alternatives

A fantasy of pain, a dream of death,
A cry of agony, a shallow breath,
Such is the world you see. Is this your choice
To be the substitution for God's Voice?
There is an Answer to all questions here,
An instant when the world will disappear.
Perceptions pass, however sure they seem,
For Christ has put His ending on the dream.[1]

CHAPTER 11

The Next Step: Application Of
A COURSE IN MIRACLES

THE TENDENCY in the human being is to be like others, to follow the trend. He complies to this most obediently and unquestioningly conforms to the belief that self-improvement is the solution to unfulfillment. He settles for the improvement of self rather than the outgrowing of it.

Self-improvement inevitably leads man to the intensification of personality — thus the greater separation from the Oneness that is Life. There are many of these deceptions in which we are caught that we do not acknowledge. The fact is, in the final analysis, very few want to change — to modify, yes, but not to be liberated from all that is of personality.

A Course In Miracles is an action of unlearning and undoing deceptions, a revolutionary action of Life upon man's consciousness. It has the power to liberate each person. It has the wisdom to remove man's ignorance and the fire to burn fear out of the life of every person who reads it. It has the truth to totally destroy selfishness and the blessing to cleanse us of all that today binds us. *A Course In Miracles* imparts the Holy Instant to free us from the old, conventional belief system of uncertainty — the unreality — and endows us with the blessing of God that makes change possible. It is life-giving.

Could you then bring *A Course In Miracles* into application? Application of the Course means that we are ready for internal action, internal correction.

Yet we are afraid of uncertainty, therefore we fill every gap in our mind with conclusions. We are in the bondage of our projections and conclusions which have become our prison. What was concluded a month ago, or six months ago, or seven years ago, or two thousand years ago, goes on. And we cannot seem to step out of it.

The truth of it begins to unfold when we do not conclude. Something else takes place — something called outgrowing. Outgrowing the past, the known. It is a miraculous moment where the undoing begins and an awakening takes place that is not of the past or of motives — a glimmer of that which is untouched by thought. And it could be called what? Extension.

Extension has its own wisdom, its own resources because it is free of thought. Something new is born upon the planet because one person came to the power of the Holy Instant, and with that, a new light, a new power, a new strength. Nothing that is of time and of personality can stop it because it is not external. It is part of creation. What can oppose it?

You are probably still giving yourself the conclusion that you cannot do it, are you not? Or that it is going to be difficult, "I wish I could do it." Every interruption of yours is corrupting you. We are victims of our own interpretations. We are not with the truth of who we are. That is *the* basic issue of man.

We need to extend who we are, not what we *should* be. We have something to do on this planet that is as vital as anything any prophet has ever undertaken: to deal with the basic issues of man. And it gives strength when you realize the importance of your function. It has its own vitality to always renew itself. And there is no imitation in it.

We need to learn to be with the new and have some space within ourselves not to conclude; and also to love uncertainty. Anything new must have the pure premise of uncertainty in it. Our constant craving for certainty and security is a block. It's the old. And that is what we have to change. Uncertainty introduces one to trust and faith in that which is bigger than personality. It, to me, is the only certainty.

We then are outgrowing the earth and its thought systems. We are coming to eternal values, some relationship with eternal laws. They are the saving grace of this age and bring a new energy upon this planet which is far superior to economic energy, to the Pentagon or Kremlin energy, or to all the energy of greed and self-centeredness.

A Course In Miracles comes with a new energy and says: nothing that happens in separation is real. The Course is not only specific in its message, but it also gives the guidelines for discovering this as fact. And now there is a yearning in man to bring the Course into application. If we would be part of this natural, next step — the application of what it imparts — we would be consistent with the Divine Forces that gave it to us. This is the need. This is what we need to learn: application.

We have never known application. Christ has said, ''Love ye one another.'' We do not know that. ''Thou shalt not kill.'' We do not know that. We know words about it. We know how to preach it and we know it as an ideal. We know that we even want it. But hardly has it ever been brought into application. In that sense, *A Course In Miracles* offers one the rarest of opportunities. It does not mystify things. It deals with the issues directly. It deals with your life.

Application, now, is a must, for you, for me. If that is our wholehearted, pure intent — if we are true to application — we will find a strength and a richness in it. If we are absolutely sincere in our heart, having given our life to application, then there are no problems. But we cannot say this *now,* and then live something different. If we do, we will suffer from our own lack of conviction because we will be forever bowing down before our weaknesses.

Our whole life has to change. We have to come to a life of integrity. There is no other choice. It is either one or the other. Are we with the old or are we with the new which is application? If we bring the old to an end, the new has begun. If we *want* the new to begin, know it will not be the new because it will be a projection. The only new thing you can do is to end the old. Then you are extending *A Course In Miracles.*

Nothing real can be threatened.

We have to live by that.

Nothing unreal exists.[2]

There is no other problem, no other issue.

When we are always preoccupied with problems how can we love anyone? How could we come to peace? Life has become so self-centered it has no space for the Holy Instant. People's lives are trampled with jobs. We are trained in schools but who has wisdom? Who knows peace? Who has love to give? Our very premise is that of lack and we live by skills. It is as if we have become beasts of burden trained to work in offices. You have no choice. You have to survive. We have not yet faced the external issues of man, where that which can be threatened rules — not trust, not reality.

And so you have to make a decision. The power of decision is yours and yours alone.

I will step back and let Him lead the way.[3]

Is this in application? The State itself would undo all that is of this world, the external which has been given to us by millions of years of fear and survival and competition and ambition. But to hear words that are eternal, you have to come to the boundlessness of your own honesty.

But you do not mind being a victim of the world. You just call it by different names in order to justify remaining the victim. *A Course In Miracles* deals with undoing these deceptions and helps you undo what stands in the way. See your tendencies, your habits, your fears. Then say, ''I am steadfast. Nothing is going to affect my decision.'' There is no seeking in it. You just undo. You undertake to deal with your own conditioned self, having the conviction that:

Nothing real can be threatened.

This Holy Instant you can come to the conviction that is not affected by time, that you will stand your ground no matter what happens.

What inner awakening, what sense of detachment, love of truth, right livelihood and purity of thought it would take to realize what is meant by bringing *A Course In Miracles* into application!

I would like to establish one premise: unless one's first love is God, application is not one's need — nor is it possible. ''My first love is God'' means that your first love is truth, that which is absolute. Is your first love God?

If we do not want to come to true relationship with God or with truth, then there is not much anyone else can do. And if we do not want to have a true relationship with God or with truth, we will not have it with our brother either.

Can we say, ''This is the function and the purpose of my life — to have a true relationship with God, with the Father — and I will honor this instantly no matter what the issue is. Wherever there is forgetfulness or lack of clarity, I will be glad to step out of it instantly.'' Therefore you are not ruled from the outside. See how simple it is.

The things of the earth are things you have projected in your images. Now you are not going to live by thought images but by love. Immediately you honor it. It strengthens one out of helplessness. It is for the one who has seen the illusion of the world.

Deception has to be laid aside. And it can be done only if it is our single purpose to do so — the purpose of bringing a truth to application.

Either your love is for deviation into conflict and problems or your love is for God. We cannot say, "God is my first love," and then have fear. Could it be possible? If there is a problem it is a misperception. Can we come back to our original love for God and correct it? Otherwise our own impurities, our own lack of clarity, our doubt and thoughts of despair remain the same. This is the correction that needs to be made.

God's Plan for Salvation is here to bring man to the awareness that there is no lack. There is only perfection. In the insanity of the world it is not possible to realize the truth that there is no lack because there is fear, survival, selfishness, self-centeredness. And *A Course In Miracles* is helping us to step out of that. It is the remembrance that "My first love is God" and God's Plan has no lack that would awaken you.

In truth, application does not require time for it is outside the realm of time. That is the truth of it. Time is something we project. Application is not of time. Alternatives need time; deviations need time. Application does not because it does not have a goal.

Thought has a goal which it pursues. And for this it needs time. Thought uses time as a means of postponement. Time prevents application. It is a technique for evading. The evasion comes in when you want to go towards learning and we are saying that mere learning does not work. It is a fallacy.

Application has no need of time, thus, no need of learning. It is instantaneous, here and now. And therefore it must be part of miracles; it must be of the Holy Instant.

When application is real, there is no time and there is no thought. Nor is there dependence or confusion. When you come to the clarity of application, you are independent of all that is external. Application means that you have come to inner peace.

How would you know if application has taken place? You would know by how you relate with your brother, how you make your bed, how you do everything. There is no other proof. How you do the things you do would tell you whether it has happened. It would have its effect on the physical experience even though *it* cannot be defined. Something in that quietness and peace takes place that stays with you and will never leave you because it is forever.

So lofty is the stillness of one's own being that nothing of the earth has much value anymore.

What can measure the nobleness of fulfillment or the ecstacy of a still mind!

This quiet is a continuous thing. It is an absolute change. It might appear to be minor but its memory comes to you when you are doing something and you begin to question: "Has this any meaning?" And somehow, it remains your companion. You can call it the Holy Spirit. You can call it by whatever name you like. But it begins to reveal in an instant that which is meaningless, that which is not real. The change would go on manifesting itself and grow in strength.

When you change, the world is changed. Situations to which you would normally react no longer have hold over you. You are declaring your freedom from the old patterns, the ego ways; you are creating a bigger gap between the thoughts. Awareness has become part of your life. You become more thoughtful in whatever you are going to say, whatever you are going to do.

Could you make quietness a part of your life that way? Could you create within yourself a yearning, a longing for that peace at all times? Could you be grateful for *A Course In Miracles*? Your inspiration becomes your strength and makes you responsible for bringing the Course into application.

There is no excuse for negligence. If there is, discover that you are unwilling. Deal with that truth. Discover your unwillingness, but do not stop there. Do something about it. Take responsibility not to drift into the old habits. You have to take a stand. It is very, very fundamental.

Helplessness and unwillingness are synony-mous. As long as they exist, separation continues. No one can end separation having these two as a law of his life. That is what we have to remove. That is the challenge.

There has to be a willingness in you that attracts this other action of awareness. You become more receptive and can say, '' 'I and my Father are one.'⁴ Whatever He Wills is alright with me.''

I hope that such a thing can take place — that you want to include the Will of God in what you do. It becomes the foundation of your life, out of which another action emerges in the world and in yourself. With that step comes constant remem-brance and touches of awareness that keep on reminding you that thought is not real, that the external does not exist. It brings you closer and closer to the Will of God.

How long it will take to find that which is true remains up to you. It all depends on your own receptivity.

> . . . this implies a willingness that you have
> not developed as yet.⁵

How much of your life you put into it is what mat-ters.

You have taken a step in that direction. There-fore, give it honesty, make it valid. And every time you do, I assure you it will be because of the quiet moment which is at work in you. It will never be otherwise.

The peace of God is shining in you now, and from your heart extends around the world. It pauses to caress each living thing, and leaves a blessing with it that remains forever and forever. What it gives must be eternal. It removes all thoughts of the ephemeral and valueless. It brings renewal to all tired hearts, and lights all vision as it passes by. All of its gifts are given everyone, and everyone unites in giving thanks to you who give, and you who have received.[6]

CHAPTER 12

What Prevents Application?
Casualness

This is a course in how to know yourself.[7]

CASUALNESS IS a great defense against truth. From time immemorial, casualness has been the issue. One could talk about fear, about attachments, about irresponsibility. One can branch out to different moods, emotions and names. Yet casualness remains at the root of them all.

People claim they want to step out of casualness, but that is as far as the words go. Circumstances change and the intent gets forgotten. That is what casualness is. When crisis comes, you project deceptive alternatives to pressure yourself and plead helplessness. Yet,

My single purpose offers it to me.[8]

We have said that once your purpose is wholehearted, the means are given. And this is what we lack. Just see what unreal lives we have lived.

A Course In Miracles states:

No one can fail who seeks to reach the truth.[9]

What can be difficult when the means are provided? If this were not so, we could justify remaining confused and helpless, not knowing what to do.

In order to step out of casualness, we must not seek illusions to replace truth. Anything that would divide one — the power of choices, the duality — can be seen as the illusion that it is.

Casualness exists when you limit yourself to thought and time. Thought and time are one misperception. The self is always of the thought. It is born of casualness because it knows nothing eternal. We have to come to a state that is not of time. This requires wholeheartedness. To . . . *single purpose . . .*[10] the means are offered to outgrow casualness. You are the determining factor.

Knowing with certainty that the means are given, you trust. Trust is not external. Like faith, it is already in you. Faith is unchangeable for it is eternal.

The conditioned thought which forms our opinions is to be questioned. Conditioning means that one is ruled by thought. We are in its bondage.

The difficulty lies in that we want to cope with casualness with thought that is itself casual. We rarely act without the use of thought and habit is the strongest enemy.

One would have to do something contrary to thought. And the energy will be given if one does not waste it on opinions. Opinions promote self-assertion. What is implied in coping with opinions?

Opinion is never complete. It is a biased and limited viewpoint. If your opinion is strong, you are in the prison of the ''I.'' You come first and therefore, the givingness of something else does not. You can then justify the laws of self-centeredness, the laws of the earth.

Goodness, however, is superior to opinion. Whenever goodness is more important to a human being than his opinion, that person has become wise. He knows what is harmonious. Harmony can only be where there is givingness. Where there are opinions, they block the giving. We can all have opinions, but very few have goodness; therefore, there is less harmony. Harmony is merited by goodness, not by opinions.

I am not saying to subordinate opinion — because denial creates other frictions — but rather, to rise to goodness. There are tremendous dimensions to goodness for it is not touched by fear.

Step by step, you would begin to say: ''This opinion will never rule me again.'' At every turn you have to make a decision. One wrong decision can determine your whole life because it starts other cycles of cause and effect. The decision of a self-centered person is always going to be in his own favor. He believes he is in control.

We do not know how to make decisions that are not self-centered, that are not for the easier side of the easy. Life, then, would intervene and compel us to make unselfish decisions through crisis situations.

[The teacher of God's] qualifications consist

*solely in this; somehow, somewhere he has
made a deliberate choice in which he did not see
his interests as apart from someone else's.*[11]

The clever ones, however, have developed a strong self-interest. They are successful for a time in deluding themselves. But they never sleep in peace.

We are to discover there are other laws based on virtue and sacredness by which to live a life of ethics.

We must doubt our own conclusions to be with the truth exactly as it is and to touch upon the wisdom that dissolves illusions.

Wisdom means that you move from honesty. But somehow, particularly in the western world, we cannot afford to do so. We need a skill to get a job; therefore our lives are not our own. We are resigned to this conformity and continue to conform our children.

We do not have our feet on the ground. Our opinions are borrowed. We do not have an original thought that is new at this moment, never thought of before.

Now here we are, and someone says: "Let go of vested interests and make God your first love. Make goodness your first love. Or make your brother your first love." And we cannot make this transition. We cannot change. Which one of us can say that God comes first? One could change the face of the earth if one's first love were his brother. We have to see something else that shines in the brother, that is more than the flesh and more than the evident. The energy is there to do so. How you use it determines who you are.

When we do not use the energy rightly, we change the very vibration of the planet. Higher values and ethics have all but disappeared. There is so little sacredness left. And today the whole of humanity itself is threatened.

The casual mind is hardly aware that decadence is upon us. Do you not see what has happened to us? We have become money-minded. This is what I mean by decadence: constant calculation. The casual mind is already highly conformed, and it contributes to the decadence by giving power to those who monopolize. This decadence is appalling.

There is dictatorship everywhere — communist dictators, fascist dictators, religious dictators. There are business dictators, consumer dictators, fashion dictators. Anyone who molds your thinking is a dictator. And we are all molded and conditioned. We are made biased. People are persuaded, made to do things. Anyone who is casual can be molded one way or the other, no matter where he lives in the world.

It is almost impossible to get an education that is concerned with *your* awakening, with what you could contribute to mankind. Education today is geared to skills and survival. You are owned by the system. If you have been to a prominent business school, a corporation will pay you a starting salary of approximately sixty thousand dollars a year. But you pay with your life. The corporation dictates:

"This is the product and you have to continually improve capital sales." Your time is no longer your own. Eventually you will not even have time for dinner with your wife and children.

All of our life we have been doing nothing but compromise — till finally, we feel that compromise is the only way. All over the world there are tremendous problems. People are frustrated and isolated. Casualness has brought humanity to this. And now, there is monopoly and we are controlled. More young people today are committing suicide than ever before. Behold the product of the age of affluence and prosperity.

There is such disturbance everywhere. Words have lost their meaning. Wisdom has been replaced by armament. When you see that it has become absolutely necessary for you to confront casualness, it opens other doors.

There is a crying need in the world. How desperately the world needs you. The world needs people who are vulnerable, who live by different values and ethics — the ethics of not taking advantage, of not being victim of the choices that promote duality, of being part of rightness and defenselessness. Then you have risen to meet the need.

As you begin to find your own voice, conflict and choices end and there is certainty in your life. Certainty is so vast that it does not antagonize nor want to rule over another. The being who has his own voice protects another's virtue rather than to take advantage or humiliate the other. The voice has love in it, thoughtfulness in it, wisdom in it. It does not conform nor demand another person to conform.

The nature of love is to give.
The nature of conformity is to take.
We have to reverse this process.

Casualness, lacking vitality, is helpless, thus afraid. Being afraid, it becomes defensive and distrusting. This is the state of the world.

In what way are we going to make a significant difference?

The decision has to be made. When you get into crisis, where is your goodness going to be? Will the self still come first?

It requires real determination to make a total change in your temperament. This is how one steps out of casualness. When are you going to be responsible? At present, we want to do it but as a ritual. There is no space within. Thought will not allow it. And so, we approach change partially.

What does a casual person do? He defends himself with his thought and thus remains isolated. Are we not all isolated? We do not have relationship in the real sense. A relationship is one that does not change with circumstances. We may have mutual gratification with friends and family, but we are not related to Life. How are we then going to love one another when there is no relationship? As an idea? It will not work.

This is how serious one has to be. Do you not want to be free of illusions? The worst of all illusions — and probably the hardest to undo — is that of separation. Where there is separation, there has to be the opinion to keep it alive.

> *The ego arose from the separation, and its continued existence depends on your continuing belief in the separation. The ego must offer you some sort of reward for maintaining this belief. All it can offer is a sense of temporary existence, which begins with its own beginning and ends with its own ending. It tells you this life is your existence because it is its own. Against this sense of temporary existence spirit offers you the knowledge of permanence and unshakable being. No one who has experienced the revelation of this can ever fully believe in the ego again.*[12]

What are you determined to deal with and give your energy to? What will bring you to determination?

Discipline is necessary. Discipline means order in life. And casualness, being irresponsible, will justify any postponement.

In order to cope with casualness, one has to live according to laws which we cannot justify or pacify. We have to introduce Divine Laws into our life, some principles by which to live. *A Course In Miracles*, the Thoughts of God, is based on Divine Laws. Divine Laws are austere. You cannot manipulate them. They are the ones, however, which impart the strength. Because we are non-disciplined people, we do not value ethics. When we do not live by Divine Laws, we choose to live by casualness.

Casualness is always in turmoil. Rooted in sorrow, it can only know hate, war and destruction. The poverty and cruelty of the world where man is pitted against man and nation against nation is its effect.

Where there is casualness, there is no love. Casualness must have some psychological and physical need for another to appease its loneliness and fear. Being isolated, it exploits the other and itself. The power of its ignorance is a threat to the whole planet. The enormous efficiency of casualness is quite destructive for it separates itself from life. It is a kind of withdrawal in which we seek safety, never seeing that it is the cause of suffering.

As long as we are casual, collective consciousness will acknowledge the "me" and the "you" — and separation is maintained. According to *A Course In Miracles,*

> *The separation is a system of thought*
> *real enough in time,*
> *though not in eternity.*[13]

Casualness promotes separation; awareness undoes it. Awareness is of love and opposes no one, for love is never threatened. The issue of insecurity is outgrown. Nothing of thought, fear, jealousy or antagonism has the power to affect it. It is a state untouched by problems. The man who has discovered his potential knows what love is, what truth is. He has received the Gift of God to share. Out of his power of stillness, the new is born upon the planet.

*Knowledge is not the motivation for learning
this course. Peace is.*[14]

When you are at peace, you extend peace. The
conflict has ended within you. That wholeness is
independent of the externals, for the external is but
illusion. The external is but the past. It is all
images.

The power that is not of time — the power of
love, truth, forgiveness, gratefulness — does not
oppose anything because there is nothing else.
What would it oppose when it sees only the Grace
of God? It is innocent of all things that are unreal
because they are projected.

It is a direct expression of the Will of God that
manifests when one is whole. The Will of God then
does its work through you. If you do not have
preferences, you will not deviate from it. You will
not oppose it. You then have the means to be ever
quiet and peaceful.

You will know your function and what you are
doing will be consistent with the Will of God. This
is the one thing casualness does not know and will
never know.

In the quiet, holy instant of wholeness, one
comes to gratefulness for His action of Grace, the
shared purpose of extending His will upon the
earth.

CHAPTER 13

What Prevents Application? Resistance

H OW DIFFICULT it is to communicate the Real, with all the non-real things we know. "Knowing" becomes terribly detrimental when it intrudes upon the stillness of the mind and obscures the living reality of *now*.

What is real is to see the false as the false. This brings about a discontent within which nothing can pacify. Unless we come to this state, we will not know how to cope with resistance. Today we are at such a low level of energy and interest that we choose to compromise rather than to face the resistance. To the degree that we can pacify and compromise the discontent within, to that degree there is resistance to knowing what is true.

What is it that maintains resistance? As long as we compromise, we have resistance. As long as our mind can formulate a problem we are planting seeds of resistance in our consciousness. Problems are self-centered; we are engrossed in our preoccupations and live by self-centeredness, remaining casual and superficial.

Who has a thought that is eternal and thus has become creative in the real sense? That thought would affect mankind for generations and centuries to come.

But we are only interested in more information about something. Learning *about* things is always abstract.

Our span of interest is very short and makes the body busy, giving the illusion we are getting somewhere. Getting to the job or getting to a conclusion are both the same. They give a false sense of achievement.

What *A Course In Miracles* offers has nothing to do with achievement; therefore, we have resistance to it. The Course states that our origin is Divine. There is nothing else to teach. Can we see that on one side there is the lifestyle of achievement and on the other, the Course which reminds us that we are perfect, that we are blessed as a Son of God? To realize this requires giving up the achievement binge. The resistance is in giving it up.

Our interest is not in our identity with God; it is in personality and how to amuse it. Do we have the honesty to see that we love the stimulation of efforts — the doings, the activity, the projection, the pursuits? To these we have no resistance. This is insanity.

There is no end to our wanting to know *A Course In Miracles* — but as abstract knowledge, not as an actuality.

Not until we stop projecting and pursuing will

we come to the stillness, independent of resistance, which has the capacity to receive the boon inherent in the Course.

To be still means the body activity and mental projections do not intrude. To be still is to know:

I am not a body. I am free.
For I am still as God created me.[15]

And we receive the Unasked.

Stillness is creative for it is part of the Mind of God. Brain activity, however, knows no holiness, no wholeness. Being fragmented, it divides itself further and further. No wonder we are who we are — fearful, self-destructive creatures.

Thought rules human consciousness. We are never free of it. Resistance is manufactured by thought.

Have you ever questioned why you have resistance? Why is there not resistance to doing a routine job that is dull and meaningless? Is there not some inherent resistance because we have not brought the principles of the Course into application?

In order to know why there is resistance, we must come to a crisis which cannot be pacified. But we evade crisis because we do not want to expose ourselves. We play it safe by remaining intellectual. Find out what your real interest is. Is it self-centered? Can you afford to be honest?

To take the next step out of self-centeredness would be the beginning of a new era for each one. If you could be a friend to yourself, you would want to free yourself from deceptions. Why is there resistance to seeing self-deceptions? We have to recognize them in order to dissolve them.

Are you willing to renounce the world of illusions? This is the real meaning of renunciation: the giving up of attachment to the deceptions by which we live. To the degree we love our deceptions there is the resistance to what is true. It is an internal issue. God's Plan for Salvation — *A Course In Miracles* — deals with the internal issue.

Internal questions arise when you are in crisis. It is a constant internal process of self-knowing. Observe that if there is fear, you go for activity; but action is impersonal because it is of Life.

Life is impersonal but we are constantly making it personal with our likes and dislikes. We have to deal with the human issues not personal problems. Human issues are common to all mankind — fear, hatred, insecurity, loneliness.

As long as we can manage without resolving these issues, there is no interest in truth. And so, we hear truth partially and learn nothing. Do you see the contradiction? We accept the false, the artificial, while resisting what is real.

We must come to a determined effort. We have never made the call to the Holy Spirit — that we want to be honest, that we want to be part of Absolute Goodness, that we want to lead a life of virtue. If we had, compassion and forgiveness would be part of our life from this day on. We have never demanded that strength of ourselves, though we have it.

Without silence, the mind becomes bound to time, to thought, to the earth, to the flesh. The only thing that is real is what you *are*, not what you *think* you are, not what you defend or promote. What you really are is far beyond the circumscribed life you live. You are an extension of Love.

When words are spoken from the Mind of God, then a creative action takes place within one. It is independent of all resistance. It is the joyous sight of a world in which there is no separation, where there is no "you" and "me" anymore. This Absolute Goodness, the action without consequences, would lift you out of the self.

A life without consequences is called "The Path of Virtue." Out of this would blossom an eternal flower born of man's fulfillment. It is his fulfillment that brings the Kingdom of God to earth. Anyone who has come to the truth of it has received it for everyone because minds are joined. It affirms that you who read it are of Divine Origin. This is one of the most powerful statements made upon this planet. And it is for you.

When a human being upon this earth speaks from the Mind of God, he sows a seed that introduces another to his eternity. It is not knowledge. It is the most blessed moment, a benediction.

Such a being is the messenger of Gratefulness. He then can introduce us to:

I thank my Father for His gifts to me.[16]

It is possible to receive the gift of the Mind of

God. And you discover that in your stillness, you are one with Him.

A Course In Miracles is the Thoughts of God, the Mind of God speaking to you. The creative vitality of its words will remove all resistance. It is a contact with the Holiness of Life.

This is the wondrous glory of *A Course In Miracles*.

CHAPTER 14

What Prevents Application? Unwillingness

The holy instant is the result of your determination to be holy. It is the answer. The desire and the willingness to let it come precede its coming. . . . Trust not your good intentions. They are not enough. But trust implicitly your willingness, whatever else may enter. . . . The miracle of the holy instant lies in your willingness to let it be what it is. And in your willingness for this lies also your acceptance of yourself as you were meant to be. . . .

The holy instant does not come from your little willingness alone. It is always the result of your small willingness combined with the unlimited power of God's Will.[17]

NO ONE CAN end separation as long as unwillingness is the law of his life. No matter how virtuous or how sincere we want to be, it will never work as long as our lifestyle is based on unwillingness. There is no way out of it. Unwillingness is THE factor. This is what we have to remove. This is the challenge. Just to know this is worth a lifetime!

Our lifestyle is that of unwillingness to change. Every single person. All problems emerge out of unwillingness. There is no other problem. All through the ages, everyone has had the same issue of unwillingness to change.

No one needs to feel inferior or superior. Every single person who is separated lives by the law of unwillingness. That is what maintains the separation. And it is the hardest thing to confront in oneself. Even when *A Course In Miracles* says, . . . *he goes with mighty companions beside him,*[18] the fact remains that you still need to deal with the unwillingness in yourself. This is a fundamental law. If a man can overcome that in himself, he is indeed a unique being — one who merits being called a teacher of God.

Unwillingness is always unfulfilled, always unhappy because its whole premise is of lack. Therefore it keeps itself busy; it will always find some reason to postpone. The unwillingness itself creates unresolved issues which consume a lot of time and energy and bring in constant delay. It uses these issues to divert the attention. It is ever evasive; it plans this, believes that, all in order to deceive itself. It wants not to be unwilling, to overcome it, but it makes sure never to change its unwillingness. It will even become religious: say the rosary, meditate, do yoga. But the unwillingness is still there.

Can we discover that ours is a lifestyle of unwillingness always *wanting* to be willing? Where there is unwillingness, there is the *becoming*. Where there is becoming, there is the self-centered activity of *wanting*. Where there is wanting, there is confirmation of lack, of unfulfillment. And that is what one extends. One is never free of wanting. Change is not a wanting.

We must face the unwillingness that does not want to deal with the internal issues. Millions upon millions of people evade them. And out of one million or ten million, if there is one person who succeeds, he will have brought *A Course In Miracles* into application.

Is there the remotest chance in this lifetime that you may overcome unwillingness? The choice and the decision are yours.

The power of decision is my own. [19]

We are convinced by the belief that we are helpless, weak, and cannot cope. Helplessness wants "the Lord to do it." But the Lord does not make anyone dependent on Him. He says, ". . . the works that I do shall he do also; and greater works than these shall he do . . ." [20] It is up to *you* to overcome unwillingness or not.

The fact is that because we are passive and indifferent, we have not made changes within ourselves. We are not truly interested in bringing anything to completion. We are so primitive. Primitive, to me, means that we are not fired with a passion to change and end the separation. We do not want to come to decision; we have neither love for clarity nor the backbone of conviction.

If you do not have confidence in your ability to

change, you will not make the necessary demands of yourself to do so. We need to make a demand on our unwillingness, on our laziness and confusion. Then it becomes a strength. It requires one hundred percent of our interest — not ninety-nine. There can be no compromise. If this is not clear to you by now, it is because you are using unwillingness as a criteria, as a means of postponement. We are undertaking to confront the unwillingness that prevents man from changing.

> *I need add nothing to His Plan. But to receive it, I must be willing not to substitute my own in place of it.*[21]

So far unwillingness has been seated on the throne. It has kept us the way we are. Unwillingness extends unwillingness. And the change only takes place when unwillingness is no longer in charge of your life. Only when willingness has come into being does a change take place.

If you are really earnest, God's Plan for Salvation will be there to strengthen you. Life would help you. It has already helped you by making this clear. Willingness is brought to flowering and it becomes a fact in your life. There are no options to it. It is now a certainty. The gift of responsibility, the gift of certainty — these gifts God's Plan for Salvation has to offer you.

Then you can say:

> "I am true to who I am.
> The blessing, I receive.
> The blessing, I am.
> The blessing, I extend."

Part 4

My Father's House

Hallowed my name. I am a Son of God
Who walks in stillness. I hold out my hand,
And from my fingertips the quiet goes
Around the world to still all living things,
And cover them in holiness. Their rest
Is joined in mine, for I am one with them.
There is no pain my stillness cannot heal,
Because it comes from God. There is no grief
That does not turn to laughter when I come.
I do not come alone. There walks with me
The Light that Heaven looks on as itself.
I am a Son of God. My name is His.
My Father's house is where my stillness is .[1]

CHAPTER 15

The Teacher Of God

THE TEXT AND *Workbook for Students* of *A Course In Miracles* have introduced us to who we are — that we are spirit created in the image of God. They have given us the means to make our will one with God through forgiveness and the ending of grievances and attack thoughts. They have spoken of the undoing process and dealt with the issues within each person. The *Manual For Teachers* speaks directly to those who respond to the call to be a teacher of God.

What is the function, the role of the teacher of God? By what laws and ethics does he live? What is his relationship with people? What does he impart?

The teacher of God must make his will one with God. Only by being the extension of that Will is he then the teacher of God. What prevents him from being one with the Will of God? And can he be a teacher of God if he is not? The challenges are now before him.

Obviously, he has to do a lot of ground work in his own life, sorting out the false. He has to change his values and come to wisdom and simplicity. All of these things must he do to have a life that is more consistent. Although it is not yet the extension of the Will, the atmosphere is created for what the Course calls "Atonement" to take place in his life. The energy is there to be with what is authentic rather than ideas. The outgrowing brings about a change in his intent, his values and his life. The world of circumstances and attraction no longer sway him.

Although these things have taken place, the Will has not as yet become one, for that can only occur when he begins to teach.

Herein is found a very subtle point. The teacher of God cannot wait until he has made his will one with God before he begins to teach. The Course makes it very clear that the teacher now needs the student for his own sake because only then can he himself learn. There is no other way. It is a paradoxical phenomena that he becomes the student as he becomes the teacher.

We must understand certain laws, keys about Life and creation.

First there was the Word. In the beginning there was no manifestation, just one tremendous seething sea of life. Let us call it the potential. The potential existed although it had not yet expressed itself in action.

Then, out of God's compassion, He expressed; and all that is Real was created, became His expression — the Son. And it became a potential anew to receive what God had to give. Out of that, Creation was born.

For example, when a woman becomes a potential she receives the seed of man and creation then comes into being. Being the potential, she receives. Let us call this that receives, the "feminine."

When she has received, an action takes place: she creates and something gets completed. It is the miracle of the potential becoming an Action — or creative. Let us call this that acts or is creative, the "masculine."

This can be observed throughout. The earth is a potential. It receives the water, the creative action, and then comes into activity, into creativeness. You see it as well in a tree. It is first a potential, and then it produces seed and fruit.

It is a principle of potential/receptivity/feminine versus action/creativity/masculine that is to be understood. Similarly, as teachers of God, we must come to the potential in order to be ignited with the Will.

Let us see how this takes place.

The student asks a question which the teacher of God cannot answer — for the answer is not based on anything known. In order for him to receive the clarity, the teacher must come to love in which he wants to help the other.

Thus, a need is created. The teacher has become a potential to receive and the clarity is given to him instantly. It is the clarity that is the extension and that continues. Therefore it is neither the teacher's nor the student's. Clarity is the first cause. It can come as an answer or it can come as an undoing. But the teacher cannot receive it unless he becomes a potential; and he cannot become a potential unless he creates a need. The teacher receives and then he gives. Thus, both the teacher and the student receive. There is no other way for the teacher to receive except by giving.

As a potential, the teacher is feminine. To the potential is given the clarity to impart. The minute he becomes the teacher and imparts, he becomes the masculine. So, to God, the teacher is feminine; to the student, he is masculine. Somewhere, then, there is always the shift of polarities.

When the teacher responds to the need of the other he also discovers a state of love within himself. Love is the potential. Therefore, he has to come to love.

To teach intellectually is devoid of love. In it there is no real teaching-learning relationship because God is not involved. It is but the intellectual accumulation of knowledge — and nothing new can take place or be received.

One is boundless and of God; the other is what you have been conditioned by and have accumulated. One is personal; the other is impersonal.

Knowing this first premise — the teacher of God being the potential in order to receive — we then must discover: What is his function? What are his ethics? What are his incentives? What makes him a teacher?

Invariably, the teacher of God has come to a point in which he realizes he has no options. He has understood that there is nothing else he can do. Everything he has done has brought him to this point of recognition. It is not merely a momentary decision. He has found what he is to do and it relates him with God, with Love, with man and with action.

What, then, is he going to teach? In actuality, the teacher of God has nothing to teach because in the potential there is no expression. If he were to teach his own limited knowings and conclusions, he would be a false intellectual teacher. This kind of teaching must be outgrown. Can he keep himself empty? Can he be so strong a potential that he can receive?

The function of the teacher of God is to come to an intensity of receptivity which is not a knowing. What the earth really needs, and a teacher has to bring, is something of God. In this way the teacher makes his will one with God. It is a simple loving act in which he becomes the co-creator. There is no striving in it.

Are we beginning to see the all-encompassing importance of "Love ye one another?" It is a relationship, a continuation of the action of Creation. To love another would be to care enough not to give him something of the known, but rather to introduce him to something of Heaven, the new.

He gave just one commandment: "LOVE YE ONE ANOTHER." It is a law, not an idea or a concept. The survival of man depends on it.

Having seen the illusion people are caught in, what does a teacher of God do? *A Course In Miracles* says the teacher of God cuts time. And nearly everyone is caught in time.

> *This is a manual for a special curriculum, intended for teachers of a special form of the universal course. There are many thousands of other forms, all with the same outcome. They merely save time.*[2]

Remember this, *They merely save time.* You can read and study all the books you like, but does it save time or is it lengthening time? Go through the gymnastics of Yoga, where would it lead? If it leads you to having siddhis[3] to attract attention to yourself, then has it not been a curse rather than a blessing?

Only at the time level is there experience which is always of the physical senses. We get caught in time because we want to repeat experience. The experiences of yesterday become important and we project a tomorrow to repeat them. One has to see the deception of time.

Can the teacher of God overcome experience? Does he feel a sense of loss when something of time is taken away from him? If he has not come to a deliberate choice, he will be weaker in the face of the bewitching beauty of success, of the raising up of the ego to great prominence — all things that weakness feeds upon. He must come to not valuing anything that is of time or experience; only then is he in a timeless state and therefore, a potential.

These are the qualifications of a teacher of God.

The teacher of God is not in the bondage of time. He has a relationship with the eternal.

Cut through time and come to eternity, for that is where your home is. That is who you are.

The ending of time in the individual life is a major step. When time ends on the earth plane, we are no longer bound to it. See what the Course is saying; it is profound:

> Yet time has an ending, and it is this that the teachers of God are appointed to bring about. For time is in their hands. Such was their choice, and it is given them.[4]

You are the master of time. You are HIS teacher and therefore you represent Him. God might be abstract to you, but love and goodness are not. Extend that. That is consistent with the Will of God as well as with your own will. When your will has become that, then you have ended the cycle of time.

If we do things that are horizontal — the worldly things, so to speak — then our source, the word that is given, is the one from the brain. If we remain with brain thought, then we have not the need to be co-creator with Him. Then you have also chosen to be separated and remain isolated, a victim of ambition and violence and all the rest.

All things are lessons God would have me learn.

A lesson is a miracle which God
Offers to me, in place of thoughts I made
That hurt me.[5]

Can we rejoice then for the daily lesson and discover the miracle that constantly brings freedom from the body and dissolves what the body projects? A miracle is that moment which is not subject to time or space. As long as we want body experiences, we are bound to the concepts of time, space and body senses. This is our choice.

> *What I learn of Him becomes*
> *The way I am set free. And so I choose*
> *To learn His lessons and forget my own.*[6]

The forgetting of one's own lessons is essential to the learning of His. This transformation takes place in the one who is to be amongst the Ministers of God.

When the body wants no experience whatsoever, then the brain becomes still to receive and uses the body to implement what is of God. He is amongst the Ministers of God for he brings the Kingdom of God to earth.

> *A teacher of God is anyone who chooses to be*
> *one. His qualifications consist solely in this;*
> *somehow, somewhere he has made a deliberate*
> *choice in which he did not see his interests as*
> *apart from someone else's. Once he has done*
> *that, his road is established and his direction*
> *sure.*[7]

The teacher of God makes a deliberate choice to care as much for another as he does for himself — and the separation begins to end. There is no longer "me and mine." It is a different response which one has to learn. Unless he can lose sight of separate interest, he cannot teach. Yet the minute he takes the step he becomes an expression of the soul rather than of time. A miracle has taken place and has cleared the way for His Will.

It is the teacher of God's responsibility to find out what the forces are that prevent him from making another person's interest his own.

The Course points out that a teacher of God must not judge. Judgment does not recognize that the other person is made in the image of God. Could you never deviate from seeing the reality of what God created in another being? Then you have outgrown experiences, time values, loss and gain and reactions.

Is there the burning fire in you to come to some discovery and say, ''This is what I want to outgrow!'' Is one's prayer really to the Lord to make one fit for service and not for advantage? Is this the yearning within, or is it the quest for security?

The teacher of God brings his life to a consistency, where he does not function according to time's dictates but rather from rightness. He has no vested interest. Attachments have disappeared. His relationship is with Life.

This is the choice you make. The power lies in your choosing. Can you come to this decision? Only this matters. If you limit yourself to littleness and value problems as real, then this is the choice you have made.

Be not content with littleness. . . .

There is a deep responsibility you owe yourself, and one you must learn to remember all the time. The lesson may seem hard at first, but you will learn to love it when you realize that it is true and is but a tribute to your power. You who have sought and found littleness, remember this: Every decision you make stems from what you think you are, and represents the value that you put upon yourself. Believe the little can content you, and by limiting yourself you will not be satisfied. For your function is not little.[8]

The minute you choose, you have invoked for all times the Divine Presence that would accompany you. What more could you ask for?

CHAPTER 16

The Voice Of The Ego

W E WOULD LIKE to talk about the manner in which we correct problems. Correction is an action independent of time that occurs in the present. Correction can take place instantly at any time. It is a tremendous process of awakening for it is not deceptive.

We can surely understand that we are seldom in the present, always drifting into the past or the future. The intensity of being present is where the ego never enters, indeed cannot enter because the ego is the domain of illusions. And the present deals with facts.

It is necessary, then, to understand the intrigues of the ego that prevent us from being present. This is the training we need and this is the training *A Course In Miracles* provides. There is no getting anywhere, no becoming; it is an undoing.

We identify only with the thought system of man — the self-centeredness of the ego. And we have gotten used to the gratification of sensation. We have developed a certain routine, certain habits that are gratifying; and to take care of any habit is going to require all we have. But we have the strength when it is our own inner calling to do so — when justifications and compromises no longer apply.

A Course In Miracles offers a curriculum that is consistent with our Reality, not with our conditioning. But its curriculum can be learned only when it is your will to do so, when you are not influenced or conditioned by anyone else. It will not be easy to put another curriculum into effect unless we are already disillusioned.

Self-honesty is the most beautiful gift you can give yourself for it takes great wisdom to dissolve deceptions. It is going to take a real determined effort. You have to be very earnest. Are you willing to do so?

If you have the need, the Heavens would meet it. And with the coming of *A Course In Miracles,* that need is met. It is a gift of God to you in which you begin to undo until you are totally freed of all knowings, of all that limits you.

If you have made the decision to know God, to know Love, to know Peace — then it will be given you. The Course gives an answer in words, but also it imparts another state of being. It is like a light of eternity in which conflict ends. We have to get our own self out of the way, for truth and clarity are not personal.

The self, or consciousness,

 . . . *is correctly identified as the domain of the ego.*[9]

Your relationship with yourself is based on the assessment of the ego about who you are. The ego will have you believe you are no good. Whether you get depressed by it, you feel inadequate by it or you feel proud of it, know that it is the voice of the ego. It has nothing to do with truth. It is but your opinion about yourself.

You have to see that it is the ego that tells you who you are: how wicked you are, how bad you are, how good you are. But according to *A Course In Miracles*, it is all an indulgence. To step out of it is to realize the truth that that is what the ego would have you believe.

There is no other way of stepping out of it because the counter-action of stepping out is also a gimmick of the ego. To bring that movement to an end is to stop believing what the ego is making you believe. Then you come to innocence, to the unknown.

We are in the bondage of the known — the bondage of the ego that binds us with guilt and sin and the notion of self-improvement. The ego is always going to suggest thought as a means of ending the conflict. That is the approach man has accepted since prehistoric times. And it has never worked.

When we have problems, we are in the grip of thought. In order to correct the problems, we use thought again. Thought is a form of activity which is not only independent of God, but contrary to God. Whenever there is the activity of thought, invariably it is the movement of the ego. The solution to preoccupation is not preoccupation with a different name.

What will help us step out of this momentum is to slow down the movement of thought. It is an enormous undertaking because when thought is rampant and stimulated, we do not stop to remember anything else.

A Course In Miracles now and then reminds us that every half hour, or every hour, according to the lesson, we must repeat a given statement. It also gives instruction to repeat it "slowly." And there is great wisdom in that.

We make more mistakes when our thought is very stimulated. Thought develops a momentum of its own to the point of becoming frantic. Therefore, people go to drugs, to drink, or to sex; it is all, in one way or another, a release from tension. And today, man is getting more and more stimulated. The pace is getting so fast that the need is for computers and push-button technology — faster planes, faster cars and so on. We could not create that kind of hysteria if we were with the peace of God.

A Course In Miracles says to read the lesson slowly; repeat the lesson to yourself unhurriedly. *I am not a victim of the world I see.*[10] Or, *I have invented the world I see.*[11] If we could slow down enough to say this, we would be bringing in sanity.

The Course also says that if you have forgotten to repeat the lesson, never mind; from now on remember. It does not allow us to go back to the past. If you have understood this, you will never again go back to the past to solve problems.

Going back to the past is an indulgence because the past does not exist except in the memory of the brain. It is over. You do not have to relive it. Only the ego brings the past into the present. And whenever that takes place, then we are bewildered and depressed. This is not the act of correction.

The Course says: "No regrets because they are of thought. The past is over. Continue on from here." If you have understood the necessity to start from here, then you have also understood never to accuse yourself or blame another because this also is of the past.

I have invented the world I see.[12]

See the truth of this. What is the world? How do I invent it? What is implied? Is it not the ego telling you how bad the world is or how rotten you are? One or the other, that is all the ego does. Could we say, then, that that is the function of the ego?

What if one was always to undo the ego? Then you have truly learned something. Immediately you would see you are acting in the way of insanity, of thought, of your own belief. The ego is making you believe it but you can step out of it instantly.

I am not the victim of the world I see.[13]

This is your declaration of release.

A Course In Miracles says you are exactly as God created you, that He provided the protection in which you cannot be contaminated. That is the action of Love and compassion — that forever you are protected.

145

If you could recognize that you are as God created you, that you are an aspect of the Absolute and that you remain protected by God, would you still listen to the ego's dictates? Were you to fall victim again to some depression or feeling that you are no good or someone else is bad, immediately you would stop yourself and say: "But that is the voice of the ego!"

Above all else I want to see things differently.[14]

Can you be true to this and not listen to the ego and its world? It has no reality. The only reality is the world God created and the Reality God created you. You are part of His perfection. And so, the correction is made not by analyzing the problem, but rather by putting a stop to the ego's momentum. This is a healing of the totality of man. This is a healing of ignorance.

So far, we have seen things through thought, through the physical eyes. Now we see that that is a distorted perception.

My meaningless thoughts
are showing me a meaningless world.[15]

Instantly you can bring an end to it. The miracle starts to happen internally in you and you totally free yourself. You will recognize that it is the ego thoughts that are convincing you as to how inadequate you are, that you have done it again! But you will no longer accept the authority of the ego over you. You question what the ego thought is saying and therefore, a shift in identity takes place.

You may still fall victim to believing thought is

real but whenever there is confusion, any little discomfort, immediately you can correct it: "This is not of God because He knows only perfection." There is no other existence but Love. It is an awareness that thought is punishing you and you are not subject to thought; you are not subject to what the ego says. You need not be taken over now. You are still the deciding factor.

We have given charge to insanity. Therefore, we have been irresponsible. Now we are responsible for performing miracles.

> *The kingdom is perfectly united and perfectly protected, and the ego will not prevail against it. Amen.* [16]

This is our responsibility. It does not require effort. It requires a touch of awareness of what is the voice of the ego and that you are part of perfection. You can liberate yourself and a miracle happens.

We are not with God's Plan for Salvation, as stated in *A Course In Miracles,* if we do not continually make that correction within ourselves. That is our assignment: that we would not believe in the imperfection and badness that the ego is trying to convince us of. Then indeed we are . . . *determined to see things differently.* [17] Otherwise, we remain residents of the world we invented — the ego's projected world of cause and effect in which we bury ourselves and die. That is the world we are inventing — the world thought is forming — but it is not the world that God created.

We are a victim of the world we have invented.

And now we refuse to be a victim of that. Instantly it can be corrected. It has no effort in it. The correction needs no time for the seeing of it is independent of the body. That is why the correction is an independent action.

Know that your judgment, whether good or bad, has no place. So, if you have heard the truth of this, then forever you have the key to liberation.

Liberation is of God. Any other feelings are of the ego. The choice is yours to go by what the ego points out — which is of thought or the brain — or to come to a decision that frees you.

Do you not see that we are always starting a counter-movement to what God created us to be by our own opinion about ourselves, leave aside someone else having a right or wrong opinion about us? We are identified with the ego. And the ego will never let us know the Self God created. The self we know ourselves to be is not real and it is the ego that keeps it alive.

You are as perfect as God created you, and you have the protection that has never been contaminated, nor ever will be. Immediately come back to that. Refuse to believe the ego and the miracles are yours.

God does not judge or punish because He is free of the ego. And this change has been brought into your life because you are in touch with *A Course In Miracles* that liberates you from your views about yourself and your views about another, from your views about loss and gain, good and bad.

Can one make that decision, having ended the personal preoccupation of nothingness promoted by the ego? It would lead to vision of a world that you have not invented but that God created. It would lead to contact with the Holy Spirit.

> The ego is the choice for guilt; the Holy Spirit the choice for guiltlessness. The power of decision is all that is yours. What you can decide between is fixed, because there are no alternatives except truth and illusion.[18]

> Hear, then, the one answer of the Holy Spirit to all the questions the ego raises: You are a child of God, a priceless part of His kingdom, which He created as part of Him. Nothing else exists and only this is real. You have chosen a sleep in which you have had bad dreams, but the sleep is not real and God calls you to awake.[19]

The Holy Spirit's action must end time and introduce the Son of God to his eternity in which state he then remembers who he is.

The minute you have called upon the Holy Spirit, you have already punctured the illusions. Behold His gentle reminder:

> The Voice of the Holy Spirit does not command . . . It does not demand, because it does not seek control. . . . it does not attack. It merely reminds. . . . The Voice for God is always quiet, because it speaks of peace. . . . The Holy Spirit is your Guide in choosing.[20]

You can establish a relationship with the Holy

Spirit within you for the Holy Spirit is the Christ Self in you. Do not underestimate your own potential.

CHAPTER 17

Forgiveness

Forgiveness offers everything I want.

What could you want forgiveness cannot give? Do you want peace? Forgiveness offers it. Do you want happiness, a quiet mind, a certainty of purpose, and a sense of worth and beauty that transcends the world? Do you want care and safety, and the warmth of sure protection always? Do you want a quietness that cannot be disturbed, a gentleness that never can be hurt, a deep, abiding comfort, and a rest so perfect it can never be upset?

All this forgiveness offers you, and more.[21]

Forgiveness is the key to happiness.

Here is the answer to your search for peace. Here is the key to meaning in a world that seems to make no sense. Here is the way to safety in apparent dangers that appear to threaten you at every turn, and bring uncertainty to all your hopes of ever finding quietness and peace. Here are all questions answered; here the end of all uncertainty ensured at last.[22]

Do you realize how difficult it is to forgive someone? Have you ever tried? When you are really upset and think someone has made your life miserable, you will find it very difficult to forgive. *Wanting* to forgive is not enough.

At the conventional level, forgiveness is confusing because someone must do something wrong for us to have the opportunity to forgive. We believe forgiveness is part of thinking and wait for an occurrence in order to become holy.

This is the conventional sense of forgiveness. True forgiveness, however, sets everything free. It is not intellectual nor verbal. It is the benediction, the vision of the mind that sees that anything the brain knows is personal and limited. It also sees that the physical senses — and this includes the brain — only relate with the external world. In a world of duality, it knows but the *concepts* of punishment and forgiveness.

In the external world, man's physical senses identify him with the physical body. The purpose of the physical senses is survival. They are identified with the self. Psychologically, the self wants to survive. Being tribal, its approach then creates America, Canada, Mexico, Hinduism, Buddhism, Catholicism. Its world is one of divisions.

Knowing this, can you question the validity of any form of division, be it geographical, political or religious? Unless we are freed of these, we will not know what true forgiveness is.

Forgiveness deals directly with man's deep-rooted identification with the body. In order to step out of this prison of the body senses, renunciation is necessary — being unattached to anything of the world. This is the greatest wisdom for it recognizes that the external world is not real.

Forgiveness will be known when identification with the body senses ceases. Body senses are content with ideas and beliefs, for these make little demand; but they are still the activity of personality, the "me and mine" which cannot forgive the world. All they know is: "You should do this. You should not do that." It is the vanity of knowledge that condescends upon another and wants to make sure he knows you have forgiven him. How is it possible for one being to be better than another unless he is limited to status and beliefs? This is mere activity at the body identification level. Has society produced one person who goes beyond it?

Forgiveness, on the other hand, is of a still mind. When a person is capable of choosing the stillness of the mind versus the knowing of the senses, then he may know what forgiveness is.

If one does not have a belief system, can there be disharmony? When you say it is difficult to forgive another person, then have you not pitted your belief system against another's? Neither of them is right.

If we are really interested in the Love of God and want to know what is universal, we will not get caught in a belief. And every time we are unable to forgive someone, we would see that we are in the bondage of our own beliefs.

Why do we hold on to beliefs that torment us?

What has the other person to do with it? We have no right to hold a judgment over another. Whenever we believe in anything, then we must liberate ourselves from that belief.

Do not seek forgiveness; rather, seek freedom from your beliefs. You are the one who creates the bind. Do something about that. Start with yourself.

> *In the end it does not matter whether your judgment is right or wrong. Either way you are placing your belief in the unreal.*[23]

Forgiveness, then, is the flowering whereby one gives up belief. And immediately, the brother is no longer separate.

Real forgiveness, like love and truth and peace, is eternal. And the eternal does not accept what a person does in a body as real.

A Course In Miracles makes it clear that God is ever perfect and therefore, He cannot recognize imperfection. God created us perfect and He protected that perfection. And whatever we have done in separation is the illusion we are caught in. What is perfect must be perfect; and what is whole must remain whole. Were God to accept imperfection, this would imply that He Himself was imperfect. This could never be. Therefore, anything that has happened at the realm of imperfection, so to speak, has actually never happened in God's world.

> *Home of the Holy Spirit, and at home in God alone, does Christ remain at peace within the heaven of your holy mind. This is the only part of you that has reality in truth. The rest is*

dreams. Yet will these dreams be given unto Christ, to fade before His glory and reveal your holy Self, the Christ, to you at last.

The Holy Spirit reaches from the Christ in you to all your dreams, and bids them come to Him, to be translated into truth. He will exchange them for the final dream which God appointed as the end of dreams. For when forgiveness rests upon the world and peace has come to every Son of God, what could there be to keep things separate, for what remains to see except Christ's face?[24]

This is the truth forgiveness learns. It introduces one to what is perfect within. In the absence of this reality, how easily we become appeased and think we know the state of forgiveness. In fact, we know but our own interpretation of forgiveness.

The state of forgiveness clears away the deceptions of our interpretations. It does not get into the world of reactions and grievances which are unreal. Within the world of unreality, we want to know forgiveness. Is it possible?

This, however, can only be seen with a still mind in which the brain activity has ceased. Then the light has dawned and nothing is external to you. How could there be judgment and non-judgment, "forgiveness" and "non-forgiveness," when you are vast and unlimited?

Who wants to come to that state of forgiveness? You will be risking everything you think you know by having to come face to face with fear and survival. It demands more than mere adjustments. Is your interest in survival or in forgiveness?

Who wants to know the actuality of what forgiveness is beyond definition, in which you are never regulated by thought that sustains fear?

It is not possible to forgive at the level of thought. Forgiveness has no consequences and so it is independent of thought. Can you yourself come to a moment of intensity that is independent of thought? Can you become that receptive and receive what forgiveness is? Is there that kind of intelligence — a new awakening that discovers reality and therefore dispels the thought system?

Forgiveness means: freedom from self. Where there are two personalities, they cannot forgive. The minute you are with personality, you become idea-bound because physicality is conditioned. And without knowing it, there is prejudice. You have ideas about people you have never seen and you set conclusions about them. Neither your belief nor another person's belief knows what reality is. And you and I can set out to kill an enemy we have never seen. What could be worse?

As long as you see only with the physical eyes, you think someone else has done wrong. Then you are separated from that person and from Life Itself.

> Only the body makes the world seem real, for being separate it could not remain where separation is impossible. Forgiveness proves it is impossible because it sees it not.[25]

Yet,

> A world forgiven cannot last. It was the home

of bodies. But forgiveness looks past bodies.
This is its holiness; this is how it heals. . . .

The body's eyes are therefore not the means by
which the real world can be seen, for the illu-
sions that they look upon must lead to more
illusions of reality.[26]

Illusions about yourself and the world are one.
That is why all forgiveness is a gift to yourself.
Your goal is to find out who you are, having
denied your Identity by attacking creation and
its Creator. Now you are learning how to
remember the truth. For this attack must be
replaced by forgiveness, so that thoughts of life
may replace thoughts of death. . . .

Through your forgiveness does the truth about
yourself return to your memory. Therefore, in
your forgiveness lies your salvation.[27]

The body was created to come to that purity of
forgiveness so that it could bring the light to the
world. Forgiveness is the means by which the light
of the world finds expression through us. What
greater contribution could we make? What greater
thing could we do?

Forgiveness is a religious state. It is of the Absolute — the Mind of God — which does not deviate
into physical senses. Therefore, it is universal and
cannot fit into a false, personal identity. To know
forgiveness is to know liberation from self. Freed
from self, you extend that freedom, that love. This
is your function in a world caught in unreality and
fast becoming suicidal.

We know all too well what fear and insecurity are because they are alive in us. The systems of education have activated the human brain and stillness within has become remote. Human beings are herded into schools, herded into offices. We have no real relationship with others that is not based on dependence. Where is the passion for God?

In this culture, it is man-woman relationship, rather than man-God relationship, that predominates. It centers around pleasure and intensifies the attachment to personal identity. Beyond sorrow and pleasure, what do we know?

At the sense level, there is the "you" and the "me." In the state of forgiveness, the two become the One; and the "you" ceases to be separate from "me." This is the real meaning of "Love ye one another." This is the light of forgiveness that makes of your enemy a savior.

Intellectually, we understand. But as long as we identify with the body, we continue as we are. To deal with the issues of vested interest, conclusions and conditioning requires that we come to vitality and challenge our complacency. We do not even know that there was a time when we could make an independent decision beyond influence. Today the terms are set; the conditions are laid. Almost everything we wear or eat or drink is dictated by an outside force.

Seeing the fact of it would bring light upon the land. How the light, the love, the forgiveness would express itself would be beyond belief systems. It would be the new, extending the Will of

God, as though the sun had dawned within.

Only God's Will knows what forgiveness is. And,

> *Forgiveness offers everything I want.*
>
> *What could you want forgiveness cannot give? Do you want peace? Forgiveness offers it. Do you want happiness, a quiet mind, a certainty of purpose, and a sense of worth and beauty that transcends the world? Do you want care and safety, and the warmth of sure protection always? Do you want a quietness that cannot be disturbed, a gentleness that never can be hurt, a deep, abiding comfort, and a rest so perfect it can never be upset?*[28]

A Course In Miracles is a boon which contains the blessed words that endow one's mind with strength. In every lesson of the Course, the Voice for God surrounds you and caresses you; and you receive the gifts of God to His Son.

> *Do you not then begin to understand what forgiveness will do for you? It will remove all sense of weakness, strain and fatigue from your mind. It will take away all fear and guilt and pain. It will restore the invulnerability and power God gave His Son to your awareness.*[29]

Begin to love God's world that sustains the manmade world. You will discover you are an altar of God, whose holiness blesses all things.

> *Forgive us our illusions, Father,*
> *and help us to accept*
> *our true relationship with You,*

in which there are no illusions,
and where none can ever enter.

Our holiness is Yours.
What can there be in us
that needs forgiveness
when Yours is perfect?

The sleep of forgetfulness
is only the unwillingness to remember
Your forgiveness and Your Love.

Let us not wander into temptation,
for the temptation of the Son of God
is not Your Will.

And let us receive
only what You have given,
and accept but this
into the minds which You created
and which You love. Amen.[30]

CHAPTER 18

The Real World

In the creation, God extended Himself to His creations and imbued them with the same loving will to create.[31]

Thus His Son shares in creation, and must therefore share in power to create.[32]

THERE WAS a period prior to the era of Noah's Ark known as the Golden Age or the Vedic Age. During this period were written the holy scriptures of the Vedas.

In the area of the Himalayas, there existed the great rishis or light beings — sages of another intelligence, the Intelligence of Creation. They spoke of the laws of manifestation in Creation. These sages had witnessed the drama of time-space manifestation of the planet, having themselves remained at the timeless level.

In meditation, in the intensity of awareness, one can go beyond time and space and enter into that which is beyond all concepts. Therefore, the being who is manifested and made physical can return to his original state — to Spirit.

The Vedic sages tell us that in the beginning there existed an enormous space, seething with energy. The Chinese call it a Void. What is not so readily known is that where there is energy, there is also intelligence.

In Creation, this inherent Intelligence is observable. It can be seen in the circulation of the blood, the rotation of the seasons, and the cycle of day and night. There is wisdom in existence.

And so, this great Void, this seething energy, this space, became activated and began to take form over billions upon billions of years. We are talking about a time and a space that was prior to the time-space concept as we know it. It is not three-dimensional.

The energy, in the form of dust and gases, began to move and form particles. It generated two forces: one of attraction and the other, of repulsion. Magnetic gravity slowly came into being as these particles that gravitated and rotated formed matter. Let us say that the planets came into being.

And so we see that in the beginning, there was the identity of Spirit with the Total, the All-Prevailing. Spirit did not view anything as separate because it saw beyond appearances. Not being fragmented, it saw only the One Life.

There was only bliss, a cosmic song of joy, a rhythm to everything. Spirit did not as yet have the burden of a body. For millennia it functioned that way. Through its tremendous powers, it could will anything because it was the co-creator — one with the Will of God.

"In the beginning was the Word. . . ."[33] It was the power of the Word of God that manifested everything. Spirit, as part of the vibration of the Word, could make use of its power to create. It could manifest a universe.

After long eons, Spirit became fascinated with the movement of nature, the manifested world. It was intrigued with how the Source, the Unmanifest, was manifesting Itself; and it slowly began to experiment with the manifested world and to create such things as flowers, fruits, trees and so forth. It did not as yet see anything as separate from itself.

The Spirit had form, but it was that of a shining being, so to speak. And this shining form could manifest anywhere. It did not need to project anything. But if Spirit did project wanting to be somewhere, it would be there before thought would even occur.

This went on for a long time. Then, with the dawn of self-consciousness, it began to have a sense of preference. It loved to be on the water at dawn, or to feel the relationship with the sun or the dew, the freshness and so forth. It rejoiced in this for millennia.

Gradually, however, Spirit became more and more interested in sensation. It could come into physical form and withdraw at will, for it still knew itself to be spirit.

Slowly, however, self-consciousness grew stronger as Spirit began to identify more and more with the manifested world. Spirit, or consciousness as it were, became more enamoured with his own world of manifestation and his own powers; therefore, self-conscious. With this fascination with form and sensation, there was less interest in the Eternal Voice, the communication with God. This was the separation.

> *Consciousness, the level of perception, was the first split introduced into the mind after the separation . . . Consciousness is correctly identified as the domain of the ego.*[34]

Self-consciousness had not existed prior to the separation because there had been only God-consciousness. Self-consciousness could still relate to God-consciousness and maintain communication, as between a saint and God.

> *The separation was not a loss of perfection, but a failure in communication.*[35]

> *The separation is a system of thought real enough in time, though not in eternity.*[36]

As Spirit became more and more engrossed in matter, there also emerged the first chaos: the projection of a "you" and a "me." This concept of separate identity is the most powerful, the most detrimental thing that was ever projected.

With the beginning of this separate identity, known as the individual human being, a central functioning mechanism was required, and the brain started to take form in the body. The brain became part of evolution.

Originally, the brain did not think, although it was extremely sensitive, as it is even now. And gradually, with the development of the brain, time began.

With its new physical awareness of the environment and its preoccupation, the brain observed repeated patterns in the manifested world and it projected a future.

> *We have said before that the separation was and is dissociation, and that once it occurs projection becomes its main defense, or the device that keeps it going.*[37]

And how is the future projected? It is only projected when you have past memory. Self-consciousness functions from the past, projecting a future. For example, when storm clouds come, the association is made with thunder and rain. Therefore, the brain became the storehouse of the past with its observations and experiences, always projecting a future while forgetting man's relationship with the Present — his relationship with his holiness and vastness, the eternity of his being.

> *The past that you remember never was, and represents only the denial of what always was.*[38]

Physical man has changed, being subject to evolution. But the Present has not been touched. The Present is the New that is of this minute, in which there has never been the separation into the "you" or the "me." The Present does not undergo change. Therefore, it does not know evolution or memory or separation as real.

Anything that has fragmented man and identified him with a false identity — such as dogmas and ideas — came after the separation. Today, man's culture is based predominantly on "you" and "me." Geography, philosophy, religions, politics, economy, medical systems, educational systems, all are based on the sublevel of "you" and "me." When the "you" and the "me" takes place, then you have given separation the stamp of authority.

The world you perceive is a world of separation.[39]

This idea of separateness, this conditioning is very strong.

We see that whether you are a Moslem or a Hindu, a Christian or a Buddhist, each has a way of worshipping differently. The ritual of worshipping, however, basically is the same: the separated self is "here" and God is "there." Would the wise then belong to any dogma or organized set of beliefs that separate?

It may be difficult for a Moslem to become a Hindu, which is but a horizontal change. But it is even harder for an individual to relinquish his separate identity to become a non-identity. It could occur, but it would require letting go of all the conditioning that separates.

We are limiting our horizon more and more; man is getting further and further away from the Real. Can you imagine how much we have lost in the so-called world of education and progress? We still remain uneducated. If you do not know your Self and your Source, then what is the good of it?

We worship science and education, which serve a purpose in the physical world. But these also externalize life, promoting stimulation, thus deprive us of awareness even more.

In the man-created world, stillness and peace are remote for the most part. Peace is eternal. Yet we have lost touch with our eternity. We do not know what the real world is because the real world is related to stillness and peace.

> God gave you the real world in exchange for
> the one you made out of your split mind. . .[40]

The world we know is of "me and mine," of matter and energy. It is the manifest world limited to opinions, self-interest and the self-centered activity which accumulates.How we have limited ourselves! We have lost our God-given gift of awareness.

> Yet in the returning the little light must be
> acknowledged first, for the separation was a
> descent from magnitude to littleness.[41]

Awareness is not personal for it does not fall into the realm of accumulation. Awareness is not only of this world of physicality and manifestation, it relates one to the Source beyond appearances. In awareness, there is the Presence whereby you discover your eternity, your wholeness.

The real world must be beyond thought. It is even beyond the realm of experience to which the physicality of the human being is limited through separation.

In the absence of awareness, we remain as we

are: self-centered and interested in accumulation of knowledge. And education says: "I will energize your greed and give you efficiency. Never mind love; never mind awareness or stillness or peace." And man settles for these deceptions.

Where is the urgency in our life to step out of deception? Action would be of the vitality that can no longer compromise. Why are we bound by helplessness? Have we not had enough of it?

Begin to ask profound questions, not just to be satisfied with information someone else can give you. Explore and discover how emotions came into being, in terms of creation. How did thought emerge? It is the pestilence of separation.

You might think: "What can I do in this world? What can I do alone?" Yet we have example after example that it is always the one person, untouched by helplessness, who changes history and the course of humanity.

Helpless people are easily exploited by those who live by advantages. This tendency is prevalent all over the world. Plants compete for sunlight and man, as well as nations, competes to get to the point of advantage. There can be no love or peace in competition, nor can it be said to be intelligent.

Can we come to a state that is of the real world, rather than being confined to the physicality of "me and mine"?

In this process of isolation from reality, man's relationship has become limited to that of the earth which is born of self-centeredness and survival;

and he has forgotten his Source. The man of God, however, derives his energy from the Spirit and this is what he extends.

> *Put not your faith in illusions. They will fail you. Put all your faith in the Love of God within you; eternal, changeless and forever unfailing. . . . It is your acknowledgement of the truth about yourself.*[42]

> *You are the work of God, and His work is wholly lovable and wholly loving. This is how a man must think of himself in his heart, because this is what he is.*[43]

Life invented a protection so that man could not be totally taken over by the false world. And so, part of man has always been guarded by the Divine so as not to break that link with the One Life that we share.

We are children of love and our lives are sacred. The discovery of one's sacredness is of great importance; and in doing so, we bless all life upon this planet.

A Course In Miracles says of the Son of God and the world he has made:

> *Everything he does becomes a strain, because he was not created for the environment he has made. He therefore cannot adapt to it, nor can he adapt it to him. There is no point in trying. A Son of God is only happy when he knows he is with God.*[44]

As a Son of God, you are part of His Kingdom.

This is the key.

The Son of God is the expression of love in the level of illusion in which we are caught. That Son is you.

What am I?

I am God's Son, complete and healed and whole, shining in the reflection of His Love. In me is His creation sanctified and guaranteed eternal life. In me is love perfected, fear impossible, and joy established without opposite. I am the holy home of God Himself. I am the Heaven where His Love resides. I am His holy Sinlessness Itself, for in my purity abides His Own.[45]

CHAPTER 19

Holy Relationship

C AN YOU MAKE a demand upon your-self not to accept what you *think* holy relationship is — so that something new might come about that disregards what is from the past? What *is* holy relationship?

For instance, someone comes to you with a need, a question, and you do not know the answer. But you see that Life has brought the two of you together and therefore it is an opportunity to know what Holy Relationship is. Can you come to an intensity that sees you exist upon this planet to meet the need of a brother? Is your life dedicated to his? If it is, that you naturally — without effort, without the brain — want to respond in a kind, loving, caring way. Is this not Holy Relationship?

You have taken on to meet a need that Life presents to you — someone else's need. You do not know what that need is going to be and will not go to the brain for the answer. But you *will* respond. In this urgency or total willingness to respond, one somehow overcomes confusion. You are certain about responding. *This* certainty is independent of confusion.

So, even if one starts from the brain, other things would happen in an involuntary way due to the caring that is there. Some other factor would come in so that it is not purely brain action. The very fact that one cares has brought that factor.

The brain would tell you: don't do anything that is not beneficial to you. It knows no goodness because it does not do anything without motive. Nothing it does is independent of self-interest. But when you care for someone else and you want to meet their need, this caring relates you with that which has no lack. It is independent of the brain. And that is Holy Relationship.

Holy Relationship is when you care for another more than you do for yourself. This may sound like a simple thing but it's not because as long as the "I" is there, you cannot care for another more than yourself. Unless, of course, you love deception. Put in a very simple way, there is either deception or there is Holy Relationship.

When you genuinely care for the other person and you want to meet their need, time stops. Something else takes place that is not just from the brain — although the brain can play a part in it. When you respond what occurs comes from that moment. It is the ability to be attentive. If I am interested in what you have to say, that very interest, that very attention brings something else into being. It has no motives at all. You can call it love, you can call it caring. But can you imagine that attention is what undoes motives! We have to start with being attentive and caring to undo the brain action which always has a motive.

So then, what would you say is Holy Relationship? Holy Relationship is *in* relationship. It deals with the other person at that moment. And therefore it can be with anyone you meet and can take place in an instant.

What are the obstacles to Holy Relationship? We are not going to be that attentive; we are going to make it a ritual. Then we waste time and get disillusioned because it was never holy in the first place. It is the "doing good" which is of the brain, which is again an activity and a becoming.

> *Such is the function of the holy relationship;*
> *to receive together and give as you received.*[46]

One person becomes attentive. And because that person is caring and attentive, he receives something to give. But it is even harder to find somebody who is willing to receive it. So we live a very superficial life where Holy Relationship has no place.

Have you now received what has been shared about Holy Relationship? Have you changed your attitudes, your opinions, your set of ideas? Will you bring it to application or make of it another belief?

There is the light of truth in words that are realized. We hear the words but we do not receive the light, or the truth. We think that because we received the words, we have received the light. The light is independent of the brain. Truth is independent of the brain because it is total. To be total we have to come to full attention to receive.

If we have not received the light of truth, we do not have Holy Relationship with what is shared.

> *This is the function of your holy relationship. For what one thinks, the other will experience with him. What can this mean except your minds are one? . . . your relationship is a reflection of the union of the Creator and His Son. From loving minds there is no separation. And every thought in one brings gladness to the other because they are the same.*[47]

If you see the truth, then you and the other become one. You are sharing Thoughts of God because you receive it as Thoughts of God. We all have the potentials to receive, and to give what is received. This is our function. But if it is just an idea, we will have difficulties bringing it to application.

We can now see that we do not have the ears to hear.[48] We can agree with things but that does not mean that is what we really want. All through the ages we have remained with goals and ideals, and therefore the conflict still exists in us. We do not *really* want Holy Relationship; we do not *really* want a virtuous life. As an ideal we do but as an actuality we do not. These are some of the discoveries one has to make.

We must go beyond understanding. We must come to something that is realized. When we do, we are part of 'that which is timeless. When we recognize a truth, there is no personality, there is no ''you.'' And that means you are free of the motives and preferences that all bodies have, that personalities have.

Is there anything we have really given our energy to to undo? No one can truthfully say: ''I have undertaken to live by Holy Relationship and I've seen it through. Now I have the energy and the wisdom of the undoing.'' The creative action that is extended by non-personality is denied. It is like turning one's back on truth. Would you waste your life in half-truths?

One begins to see that bringing *A Course In Miracles* into application is a deliberate action. We are trained to *want* something — each one of us. Everything that the body's thought system knows, in one form or another, is a wanting. And wanting is one of the greatest deceptions. Our thought system circulates around wanting. Because we think Holy Relationship is something we have to *want* and therefore put energy into *getting,* we do not have the energy to come to Holy Relationship!

Please see this central point. We make a decision to live according to Holy Relationship. Then we find out that we cannot come to Holy Relationship. ''I want to,'' you would say. And then you think the wanting makes you sincere.

A Course In Miracles on the other hand, does not encourage the wanting. It says that there is another way which has nothing to do with wanting. And it is very difficult for us to accept something that exists without the wanting.

The problem lies at the level of wanting. How can you want what already is? Wanting is the central issue then. This we have to understand — whether you want God or you want gold, the wanting is the same.

Can we see that our whole thought system is built on wanting? What would it be like not to want anything, to be innocent? What purity that would be! Would you have problems if you did not want anything? Does innocence have any problems? That one split second of innocence would be a contact with eternity, a freedom from wanting. And you cannot want it because wanting evades it.

You cannot *want* Holy Relationship. If you do, you have instantly turned it into special relationship because it becomes self-centered. Then you are trying to conform to an authority you have imposed upon yourself — just a juicier wanting.

Do you not want to free yourself from this? We do not feel the need because the means of renewing ourselves would again be of a wanting. We would be using the same thought system based on wanting. Why do we not discover these deceptions? If we did, we would touch upon an energy we never knew before. And it comes to us unasked, not through wanting.

Whenever you want something, you have a name for it: a name for a feeling, a name for a person, a name for an object. Could we want something if it had no name? The opposite has an opposite name. What difference does it make? It is just a shift from this name to that name. We do not even know the difference between special relationship and Holy Relationship.

Holy Relationship is not the opposite of special relationship because it has no wanting in it. You cannot reach it through a wanting. That which does not have an opposite must be whole because it cannot possibly have conflict. If it does not have conflict, neither could it have a wanting.

A Course In Miracles points out that there is nothing to want. But you and I have become victims of wantings. That is the only thing our brain knows. See how many things wanting has introduced in our lives that are absolutely unessential and meaningless — the insanity of what is manmade. We are so busy with the wantings we cannot come to awareness. Therefore, we give reality to the past and future.

Where there is wanting, there is fear, there is doubt, there is dependence, there is lack of sufficiency. Otherwise we would not want. And we waste our whole life in the agony of lack. There is no peace and lack sustains the illusion of wanting.

If I can get what I want, then I feel satiated for the moment. Wanting may be comfortable for the moment but it has its consequences. That is why foolish people try to work things in their own favor. When you work things in your own favor, you are caring for yourself and not for another. This is irresponsibility because it is the opposite of love. An irresponsible person will suffer all through his life forming special relationships for gratification.

Can you imagine the insanity, the irresponsibility of getting lost in wantings? Do you not see how ruthless wanting is? It is always at the expense of someone else. Each person is in the service of his own wantings. Then it broadens out and we call it "my family," "my state," "my country" and so on.

Wanting cannot merit what is not of personality. It is as easy as that. This is a profound statement. *Wanting cannot merit what is not of personality.* Personality cannot merit what is not of time, not of the earth. Personality can only want things of the earth.

But to the earnest person, help is given from Above to undo *all* wantings. We have to undo *every* wanting if we are to know the truth of Holy Relationship. There are many tendencies to be overcome. And fundamentally, all tendencies are based on wantings. Discrimination, on the other hand, is based on knowing the difference between *wanting* and *needs*. Wanting is the deception. And as long as we have wanting, we have no relationship with the need that is already met. If we realized the truth that needs are already met, we would be liberated and self-reliant. Nothing external could affect us. Our lives would become productive, having something of the Kingdom to give to the earth.

Need is something that has no relationship with anything that is *other*. What does this mean? Need has no relationship with *another* because it has discovered the *One* and its holiness. When this is realized, wanting could not touch us. In fact, we would be ever grateful just seeing how needs are met. Even before we are born, our needs are provided. The mother's milk is there for the infant. The teeth are provided at the right time. Air, water, food, all are given in abundance by nature. Until this becomes our truth — that needs are met — we will not be able to outgrow the wantings, nor will we have the space to call upon the Holy Spirit and say:

> *This holy instant would I give to You.*
> *Be You in charge.*[49]

So then, what is Holy Relationship? It is a state of peace whereby you do not want anything.

> *I am content to be wherever He wishes. . .*[50]

We *must* establish a relationship with the One Who is in charge of the Process of Atonement.[51] Can you imagine anything more joyous, more sane, more pure? It is a stand of sanity in the midst of insanity.

We are more than the flesh, and stronger than the external forces. Holy Relationship has its own protection and will forever be provided.

> *And if I need a word to help me, He will give it*
> *to me. If I need a thought, that will He also*
> *give. And if I need but stillness and a tranquil,*
> *open mind, these are the gifts I will receive of*
> *Him. He is in charge by my request. And He*
> *will hear and answer me, because He speaks for*
> *God my Father and His holy Son.*[52]

Part 5

The Singing Reed

My eyes would look upon the Son of God.
For this I came; to overlook the world,
And seeing it forgiven, understand
Its holiness is but the truth in me.
The Christ walks forth in every step I take.
God shines within me, lighting up the world
In radiant joy. The Holy Spirit comes
With me, lest I should turn and lose the way.
For God has given me a goal to reach,
And has made certain that I cannot fail.
And so He gave me eyes to see beyond
Appearances and shadows. I will see
The Son of God exactly as he is.
And in that sight is all the world transformed,
And blessed forever with the Love of God.

How holy are my footsteps, which but go
To do the Will of God, Whose Son I am.
And how forever perfect is my will,
Which is in no way separate from His Own.[1]

CHAPTER 20

To Be With One's Function *(: that of ending the separation); (getting back to wholeness)*

> *There is much to do, and we have been long delayed. . . . take your place, so long left unfulfilled, in the Great Awakening. . . . This is our will. Amen.*[2]

HOW IMPORTANT it is to know one's inner calling or, as *A Course In Miracles* refers to it, to know one's function.

There is only one function: that of ending the separation. The function of getting back to wholeness has become secondary to man. He has found indulgences and outlets of greater interest. He has accumulated so much. Yet it is all nonsense.

Neither the learned man nor the non-learned man has anything new to say. There are very few people in the world who are capable of communicating with you what is born at this moment, the new. This level of communication is rare even though it is the most meaningful. It has the energies of the universe behind it. It frees you from yourself. You are then with the Real — beyond personality and idiosyncracies.

Have you ever seen clams or mussels attached to stones in the ocean? They will not let go. This is how we cling to personality, ever afraid of the new.

Being attentive can correct this insecurity; and this no one can teach you. Who else can bring about an internal revolution whereby you are not interested in self-improvement and survival? But do you dare question the falseness of the premise of self-survival?

We each have an inner calling, a particular function in the world, in the universe. We impose upon it the need for a profession, a career. The great Teacher, however, is Life. To know the Action of Life within is the inner calling. Can one then be independent of personal problems, of one's own ambition and need of survival so that the new can take place?

The new requires a different kind of mind that can travel from the vague — where it does not *know* — to the precise at a much faster pace. The distance between the known and the unknown can be bridged instantly. It is not conventional education that will lead you to this ability, nor the constant pursuit of self-improvement. As long as there is unfulfillment, it will color your life.

Can you always be with newness? It brings great humility and a freshness in which you can be attentive to the living moment.

If you stayed with the clarity of attention, you

would begin to discover a light within yourself. And your love would then see the light in the other. Nothing of the world would have much meaning after that. In fact, you would not even be loving another person because the "other" ceases. You marvel at the great benediction of Life. And you have something real to share. There is an action of Grace in your life for Life is compassionate!

In *A Course In Miracles,* it is said:

God is but Love, and therefore so am I.[3]

How long will it take you to go from the knowledge of this to the reality of it? Twenty years? Another lifetime? The Lesson of the Course serves to hasten this process, harnessing the energy of the present in order to shift from mere knowledge to the truth of the actual state.

The power of decision is my own.[4]

How can that which is of truth be difficult? What is difficult is to stop the momentum of the brain activity that forever interferes with the acceptance of truth. See the power of concepts and ideas.

Wisdom, being discrimination, would discover that truth is not difficult but that it is difficult for one not to interfere. The discovery then deals with the issue. It leaves love and truth and peace alone because these are already present; rather, it deals with what stands in the way. It is a process of undoing that which prevents us. And so, you help the brother in that way. The function is what meets the need of another. "LOVE YE ONE ANOTHER" assumes a different importance. Its source is Love, free of motives and future goals.

Holy child of God, when will you learn that only holiness can content you and give you peace?[5]

This divine Intelligence of existence is your friend. How can you then ever be afraid or insecure? Everywhere you see the Action of Life as an extension of love and perfection.

Fear not that you will not be given help in this. God's Teacher and His lesson will support your strength.[6]

A Course In Miracles is given to those who value knowing their inner function. It comes at a time when man is depleted as a result of the tyranny of the insecurity, fear and cravings of the ego. We are in the haunting bondage of the ego that maintains separation and confines consciousness to the limitations of physicality. How indoctrinated, how deeply conditioned we have become!

It is important to put energy into discovering our function. For through our function we will value what is sacred and thus, make space for *A Course In Miracles* in our lives.

The Course states:

In my defenselessness my safety lies.[7]

Self-protection is but the glorifying of separation. Therefore, it is not religious. Religious life requires the character and integrity not to be deceived by the deceptions that take place within you.

Notice how you promote separation, how you are constantly deceiving yourself and how your mind refuses to let go of fear and insecurity.

What is not love is always fear, and nothing else.[8]

The brain cannot be vulnerable. It cannot love. It does not know that by giving, it receives. And therefore it remains ignorant of anything that is of Divine Laws. The minute you become aware of Divine Laws everything in the universe helps because the function of man is universal, not of the world. Everything in creation exists for us but we have continually made ourselves small and petty-minded.

So, what then is your function? To bring to an end the personal brain activities that project experiences and regulate your life. It is not a further wanting. It is elimination of the false. It is the love of virtue and wisdom — a principle from which you will not deviate that gives you strength within. The clarity then has the vitality that brings one to the Path of Virtue. Once you are with this clarity, you have the urgency to bring order in your life. And what is order? Order is having virtue in life.

The Path of Virtue, which has no alternatives, introduces you to the truth of,

I am as God created me.[9]

How few people value wisdom, the Path of Virtue. Much of the world has given up on internal life since the advent of this modern, technological society. The internal life means a life where there is need of wisdom, not skills. In order to survive in the manmade world, wisdom is no longer necessary — techniques and skills are.

Without virtue, there is neither love nor truth. Love has been replaced with pleasure. The truth we live by has become, "I do as I please." Therefore, man remains related only to the body, sensations and gratification. But when man has developed the ability to say no to sensation, he has character and inner strength.

Yet how little internal strength we find in modern man. Why? Because strength does not come from skills and acquired, external abilities. Strength comes from clarity. It comes from wisdom. It comes from living a life of virtue.

People with skills will be a dime a dozen when unemployment becomes rampant. But where inner strength is found in the individual, there will be humanism and compassion.

So then, tomorrow, where will you go? We have abandoned the old people to retirement homes. There is hardly any real relationship because all man has thought about is what is advantageous to himself. Having uncles and aunts and mothers living in the same home as the young has stood in the way of pleasure. See what deterioration has taken place. The isolation of drugs and stimulation has replaced the strength of lasting relationships.

Yet the times are critical ahead. How many millions upon millions of people, believing that having a career is their function, will not know what to do with themselves as the external world collapses. They will have no real relationship with what is eternal.

Seeing the consequences of irresponsibility and that we have become conditioned to a lifestyle that identifies with personality, do we not want to change?

Having understood the issue totally, can we not deal with the consequences of irresponsibility? It brings in a spark of light, a confidence independent of personality.

The real function reverses external values because it relates with eternity rather than with time. It relates with Life rather than with personality. The real function is independent of any external situation — because it affects the external and is not affected by it. It is an action of Grace. When you have found your function, your values change and the insecurity of personality disappears.

One of the most important factors in one's life is to come to a point of self-honesty so that you need never compromise. And fear will no longer rule.

A Course In Miracles introduces us to the reality that we are the Son of God — an expression of Love at the level of illusion in which we are caught. That Love is the Son. That Love is you.

CHAPTER 21

What Is Of The Spirit

I WONDER IF YOU would recognize a holy being who is as vast as the universe if he passed you by? If someone introduced you to him, could you receive what he has to impart?

If you cannot receive from a saint you cannot receive from the Present, as the saint is synonymous with the Present. In fact, the present moment is the greatest of all saints, for it expresses only one thing: the benediction of God upon His children.

All things take place in the Present. The Present does not recognize time as reality. Unless you end the illusion of time, which you have manufactured, you will not know what is timeless or receive what the Present has to offer. Always absent with the preoccupation of thought which takes us away from the Present, we are caught in wishes and wantings, in yesterdays and tomorrows. We are consumed by the preoccupation of self-improvement — learning this, knowing that. Yet we remain just as ignorant and selfish, just as insecure and fearful.

Can you name one person who has a Master's Degree and say of him: "He does not know fear?" Can you name one person who holds a PhD who is no longer unfulfilled? If you could be in the Present, then you have learned all there ever is to learn.

The only function of the living moment of the Present is to express the blessings of God upon His children. You need never do anything to get it. It is here *now*. Would you believe in a God Who would deny it to you today and give it to you tomorrow? Would you call Him compassionate?

What are we doing? — forever running away from the blessings of life, from the expression of God's love every moment! It is the present moment that is alive, not the projection of tomorrow or the remembrance of yesterday.

An invention of ignorance is time. How important a part it has played in our lives. Those who have fallen into the illusion of time have forgotten their wholeness, the holiness of their being.

When you condemn yourself or criticize another, you are exposing yourself and saying that you are unaware of your holiness, that you do not know the miracle of the living moment that would bring you to silence, to ecstacy.

Fear and anxiety cannot touch the living moment — the realm of the Spirit. Nothing that is born of the earth and time can contaminate it. When you are ignorant of the Spirit, then your vision is only of the physical world of appearances.

It is sad not to have discovered one's own sacredness. Holiness is not discovered in one moment and forgotten the next. Once you have touched upon it, everything of the world becomes secondary and trivial, for you see perfection.

In that perfection, there is no fear; there is no "other." To have a glimpse of it transforms everything. The world becomes most beautiful. You no longer see a manmade world of ideas and divisions. You see Life — the glory of which transcends thought, far beyond what one could learn. You see God's Grace in everyone and everything.

A Course In Miracles explains:

> *Deep within you is everything that is perfect, ready to radiate through you and out into the world. It will cure all sorrow and pain and fear and loss because it will heal the mind that thought these things were real, and suffered out of its allegiance to them.* [10]

It is possible to hold hands with God in the living moment. Yet we choose to evade it. We invent loneliness in order to run away from it. It makes one wonder if anyone has ever been born at all, except in physicality. Those who come to the earth and remain ignorant of the Spirit that they are, are like never born.

Blessed is he who is born of the Spirit for he brings the Kingdom of God to earth. It is only through the Spirit of man that Heaven comes to earth. It is not limited to the Spirit of Jesus and Buddha. It is your function as well.

Acknowledge your own vastness. What is the

body but a cage? It is the means for Spirit to descend to earth so that those who are caught in physicality can hear His Voice even at the gross level. To the world of unreality, imprisoned by the senses, the man of God comes, takes a physical form and manifests God.

Without the man of God who brings in the freshness of Heaven and what is of the Spirit, the world is in turmoil, perpetuating war and hate and fear. Isolation predominates. No one is related to another. Where is there a marriage that lasts? Where is there real harmony in a family? Where do we live by other virtues, where man expresses the God in him? And yet we all are capable of doing so.

It is imperative that we bring about an internal change that is real. We are repeating this in a thousand different ways, hoping that someone will be able to listen, be receptive, able to comprehend and come to change within — this instant, without inventing the illusion of time.

It is the love in your heart that will bring the peace of God to you. It is not the food that you store, nor the armies you build. When the Love of God awakens in you, you will know to give. If you cannot give, then know you will also never receive.

> *Today we try to understand the truth that giver and receiver are the same. You will need help to make this meaningful, because it is so alien to the thoughts to which you are accustomed. But the Help you need is there. Give Him your faith today. . . And if you only catch a tiny glimpse of the release that lies in the idea we practice for today, this is a day of glory for the world.*[11]

You will know your worth to the degree that you can give. Giving becomes a passion with you: not of things physical, but of your love, your wisdom, your strength, your energy — the very vitality of your life that is of God.

As you start giving more, you become related to the Spirit, a God-like being who is eager always to listen to someone's aches, pains, and needs. In your giving, you will receive. In your receiving, everything is made holy. You will receive gifts of Heaven, the compassion of God. And that is what you will give to another.

And then one day, you will learn the perfection and the truth of what He said:

"LOVE YE ONE ANOTHER."

Let us learn to make our will one with God by eliminating what is unessential. It is as simple as that. Too much knowing complicates it.

Make your will one with God and do not rest until you do.

Part 6

Renunciation

You are not asked to sacrifice the good
Or the desirable in any way.
You are asked only to renounce all things
That would destroy your peace. For God is Love.
Center your thoughts on Him, and you will see
He gives you everything, with neither more
Nor less conceivable from this time forth,
And on to the eternal. Sorrow is
Inaccurate perception; pain is but
A sad mistake. Renounce but this, and you
Call unto Christ to pardon and renew.[1]

CHAPTER 22

Working With
A COURSE IN MIRACLES

''I Need But Call
And You Will Answer Me.''

If it helps you,
think of me holding your hand and leading you.
And I assure you
this will be no idle fantasy.[2]

READING THIS in the Course, have you questioned how and where He is going to lead you? What steps would there be in the leading?

What does the word ''leading'' mean? To know it would require some investment of our interest and attention. Since words are all of thought, can one be more meaningful than another?

The words we know originated out of the thought which came into being after the separation. Therefore, words but promote separation. By itself, separation does not exist. It comes into being only with thought. There is hardly a time when we are not with thought. This is how chronic it has become.

When we hear these words,

If it helps you,
think of me holding your hand and leading you.
And I assure you
this will be no idle fantasy.

we assume that He is going to lead us *to* something: to a better life, to a different situation. But what would the word "leading" mean beyond our superficial and intellectual understanding of it?

Do we question the words that we think we know? If we did, we would see that all our knowing is a violation of attention.

The word "leading," then, means bringing us to the attention that recognizes our natural state, our original nature. He is not going to lead us away. He is going to lead us to who we are as God created us. And most of us do not truly want that. Who prays for it?

We know the phrases and we would agree. But we cannot eliminate thought that is always leading us away from who we are. And so, we love to learn but we cannot bring it to application.

I am as God created me.[3]

As long as our thoughts are still misleading us, how can we pretend to know it? Ideas and concepts have no relationship with the truth. Who, then, has learned anything?

We do not as yet have the capacity or the attention to let go of what is always making us deviate from our God nature. Transformation is: coming to who we are rather than going away from it.

A Course In Miracles says,

> *I need but call and You will answer me.*[4]

Calling is something that requires a response. A baby cries, and there is a response to that cry. Calling is making that contact. A true call demands a response. If there was no need, there would be no call. So, a call is always a call for help, for affection, for love. You call, and He answers. You are not alone.

> *I need but call and You will answer me.*

We must also see that the only calling we have known is the one born out of a lack. All calls originate from unfulfillment. Yet if we read the lesson rightly, it would impart a quality of peace — peace meaning a state in which there is no more wanting.

Would peace have a need to call?
Does peace become aware that it is answered?

The action is so swift that the minute you have read the lesson title and pronounced these words,

> *I need but call and You will answer me.*

the saying of it has completed it. It happens simultaneously. The answer accompanies the call.

The answer is so swift that unless we are alert the contact passes us unaware — and we remain waiting for the call to be answered. For us it is always "going to happen." What can happen later can also happen in this instant.

Knowing the potential of this lesson would inspire one — knowing that when we call the answer is received by the time we have ended the statement,

I need but call and You will answer me.

We have nothing more to call for or want. We have received it. The statement could very accurately read, "I need but call and You have answered me."

In the last part of the same lesson, the prayer says:

You give the means whereby conviction comes, and surety of Your abiding Love is gained at last.[5]

"Conviction" is the key word here — but not as an idea. Conviction is the surety of His abiding Love. Therefore, gratefulness for the Love that precedes the lack is ever present. The Love that precedes thought is ever part of you. If that conviction is not yours, then whatever you do would maintain the illusion of separation, that you are "here" and God is "there."

We always think there is some external, superior being who can help us. But can He be separate from who we are?

Lack personalizes life. A personal life has problems and consequences. Yet Life is not personal.

If it helps you,
think of me holding your hand and leading you.
And I assure you
this will be no idle fantasy.

206

means that He would take you from the personal to the wholeness that you are.

So, what is the issue? The personal cannot call and the personal cannot heed the answer. When you are at peace, then you have a different relationship — a relationship with the wholeness. It has the discrimination to know what is false.

Then your premise is peace. And you do not let it be contaminated. Only you can do it, if that is what you want.

CHAPTER 23

Working With
A COURSE IN MIRACLES

"Let Not My Mind Deny The Thought Of God."

A *COURSE IN MIRACLES* emphasizes that all you need do is remember the Name of God and recognize your reality as His Son. It is a course in which we are given specific exercises to help us do so. Each person's commitment should be to bring this practice into being. No matter where you are, this application would be required.

One might ask, "What is the curriculum of *A Course In Miracles*?" One would have to discover the wonder and the glory of it. For the wisdom it contains is an essential gift to all mankind.

The lesson we will discuss in this chapter is:

Let not my mind deny the Thought of God.

What makes this world seem real except your own denial of the truth that lies beyond? What but your thoughts of misery and death obscure the perfect happiness and the eternal life your Father wills for you? And what would hide

> *what cannot be concealed except illusion? What could keep from you what you already have except your choice to see it not, denying it is there?*[6]

What is it that denies the Thought of God? Is it not that we believe we already know, and thus, settle for partial understanding? Superficially, there is nothing we do not know. That knowing, however, has no validity. And yet we remain caught in it. In the midst of this preoccupation, we are to break the habit and routine and come to the remembrance of something else. This ''something else'' is what the daily lesson of the Course provides.

If the remembrance does not expand within one's awareness, then the lesson remains a ritual and therefore, not a lesson at all. It is like the sightless eyes that look but do not see; or the deaf ears that cannot heed. And this we must correct.

> *The Thought of God created you. It left you not, nor have you ever been apart from it an instant. It belongs to you. By it you live. It is your Source of life, holding you one with it, and everything is one with you because you left it not. The Thought of God protects you, cares for you, makes soft your resting place and smooth your way, lighting your mind with happiness and love.*[7]

One can discover the process of Atonement at work in the lesson. Recognizing the Thought of God, one is fired with zest to give it the importance and not make it a ritual of thought activity.

The daily lesson imparts something new and

unknown to the computer brain. Like all things physical, the body and brain are subject to evolution. But the spirit is not. At the level of spirit, we work with the faculty of the mind, which is not physical, but rather, pure and perfect.

Since each minute the body cells change and renew themselves, what is it that prevents the transformation of self? We are continually conditioning the new cells with the prejudices and fears born out of separation. Thus we keep the old alive and prevent the renewal in ourselves as well as in the next generation. Henry David Thoreau said that whatever we call progress is but improved means to unimproved ends. And so, fear remains fear, ambition remains ambition and insecurity remains insecurity from one generation to the next. These have changed names and forms in the external but little improvement has been made.

There are only two emotions: love or fear. There is nothing in-between. It is not a matter of degrees. Saying we are becoming less ambitious is part of the illusion because the gradual process boosts our temperament and we remain quite satisfied. We are either ambitious or we are not.

This decision is made at the level which is independent of evolution and conditioning. Therefore, once you come to,

The power of decision is my own.[8]

then the new cells will remain new because you are not contaminating them further. This is called transformation.

But what good would it do having all this as information or even being able to speak eloquently about it? Relative knowledge has no meaning — except to be commercialized or to deceive people. Having first deceived yourself, then what you share would be forever loveless. Therefore, you have to drug yourself with the belief that you are helping another. See how the lie becomes the truth.

> *Who would deny his safety and his peace, his joy, his healing and his peace of mind, his quiet rest, his calm awakening, if he but recognized here they abide? Would he not instantly prepare to go where they are found, abandoning all else as worthless in comparison with them? And having found them, would he not make sure they stay with him, and he remain with them?*[9]

In actuality you extend what you are regardless of what you plan. If you are miserable, you extend misery; if you are joyous, you extend joy. Can you see the simplicity of this? We plan when we do not have the resources within. Generally, helping another is something we plan ahead of time and when we want to implement it. We project the illusion of ideals and these we seek to fulfill. But there is a state where an extending takes place which has no ideals at all. It just is.

> *Eternity and everlasting life shine in your mind, because the Thought of God has left you not, and still abides with you.*[10]

What comes unasked must be left. The less interference in it, the better.

> *Deny not Heaven. It is yours today, but for the*

asking. Nor need you perceive how great the gift, how changed your mind will be before it comes to you. Ask to receive, and it is given you. Conviction lies within it. Till you welcome it as yours, uncertainty remains. Yet God is fair. Sureness is not required to receive what only your acceptance can bestow.[11]

The lesson of the Course brings a tremendous responsibility. If it does not bring one to the challenge, then we will do the lesson but as a ritual. We may be inspired by the lesson, but it is still verbal if we have not met the challenge each lesson represents.

Ask with desire. You need not be sure that you request the only thing you want. But when you have received, you will be sure you have the treasure you have always sought. What would you then exchange for it? What would induce you now to let it fade away from your ecstatic vision? For this sight proves that you have exchanged your blindness for the seeing eyes of Christ; your mind has come to lay aside denial, and accept the Thought of God as your inheritance.[12]

This is the challenge before us with this lesson. If we recognize the challenge, only then can we take the responsibility of knowing what the lesson means beyond the words.

Now is all doubting past, the journey's end made certain, and salvation given you. Now is Christ's power in your mind, to heal as you were healed. For now you are among the saviors of the world. Your destiny lies there and nowhere else. Would God consent to let His Son remain forever starved by his denial of the nourishment he needs to live? Abundance dwells in him, and deprivation cannot cut him off from God's sustaining Love and from his home.[13]

The lesson demands seriousness. Otherwise, we resort to the learning of words, the brain activity. See how this contradiction exists in our life in relationship to the lesson.

We cannot bring our mind to stillness because we have not accepted the overwhelming challenge each lesson presents. If we persist with our thought, then are we not denying the Thought of God?

There is enormous responsibility. Are we now reading the lesson with the newness of the moment? Then we accept that challenge and become responsible. One cannot just read it and then put it aside. We must be able to actually bring it into application.

Practice today in hope. For hope indeed is justified. Your doubts are meaningless, for God is certain. And the Thought of Him is never absent. Sureness must abide within you who are host to Him.[14]

The lesson brings one to intense yearning for the Thought of God if we cooperate with it.

This course removes all doubts which you have interposed between Him and your certainty of Him.[15]

The power, the benediction and the blessings are upon this lesson. And if one stayed with it, it would impart what one needs to be free of thought. The lesson actually activates the power of the Thought of God.

> We count on God, and not upon ourselves, to give us certainty. And in His Name we practice as His Word directs we do. [16]

The gifts of God are there for one to no longer be subject to the brain activity, to no longer live in separation.

So then, what is the gift?. . . That which is unknown and will ever remain unknown to the human brain. It would be something very energetic, very different.

> His sureness lies beyond our every doubt. His Love remains beyond our every fear. The Thought of Him is still beyond all dreams and in our minds, according to His Will. [17]

In that state one wants nothing. Everything has been provided. And for this one is full of gratefulness. Out of that gladness there is an exuberance that cannot be put into words.

When one has no other need, then one is out of physicality, out of the ''me and mine.'' The Thought of God is the only thing that remains. You are out of unfulfillment and insecurity. From your boundlessness, your blessings surround the world and everything that lives and breathes upon it.

You cannot fit the Course into your life. You have to fit your life into it.

Will you give *A Course In Miracles* the space?

CHAPTER 24

Working With
A COURSE IN MIRACLES

"I Am Under No Laws But God's."

START WITH A simple question: Are there any other laws but God's? If we assume there are other laws, then we put ourselves on a false premise for *there are no other laws but God's.* There are manmade rules, but these are not laws.

Lesson 76 of the Course begins:

I am under no laws but God's.

We have observed before how many senseless things have seemed to you to be salvation. Each has imprisoned you with laws as senseless as itself. You are not bound by them. Yet to understand that this is so, you must first realize salvation lies not there. While you would seek for it in things that have no meaning, you bind yourself to laws that make no sense. Thus do you seek to prove salvation is where it is not.[18]

Intellectually, we can accept this. But we remain controlled by manmade rules under which we live.

In this there is inconsistency. We do not know what God's Laws are, leave aside being able to say,

I am under no laws but God's.

Man did not make the days and the nights, nor the heart that beats. It is not democracy or socialism or capitalism that makes the nails grow. It snows and the law of the arrival of winter is the Law of God.

Manmade rules, for the most part, are based on insecurity and fear — rules to tax you and I, certain restrictions necessary for society to function. But these rules are not laws. They are just common sense.

How seldom we live by God's Love, by God's Laws. How unaware are we of them or even grateful for them. Can you appreciate just the perfection and the intelligence of the eyelids? Just to see the function of one's own body, or the growth of a tree would bring one to a silent mind. Everything is related and extends from the joy of being what it is — an extension of the forces that focus unto it.

There is a law of extension. Under the Laws of God, everything extends and creates because everything is one life extending itself in many different forms, shapes and facets. But it remains the One Life. Nothing is outside of it; and in it, everything is in harmony.

Yet we are caught in the world of consequences. Once fragmented, our perceptions are distorted and we see only the phenomena, the appearance, and not the interplay of the One Life, the glory of it beyond time and space.

Within time and space, we cannot see Reality. We must come to our own infinity, our own vastness. Yet we have such low opinions of ourselves and are bound by limitations we have accepted as real. How then can we see the glory of creation when we have problems which consume us?

I am under no laws but God's is not merely a verbal statement. Laws of God are eternal, just as you are eternal. Why do we have such difficulty in believing we are timeless? What a misfortune that we do not know our own sacredness, yet continue to search externally for what we think we have lost.

The Laws of God introduce one to freedom. We must question things of time and thought and really see they are all illusion born out of a desperate need to be somebody and to deny we are already perfect. When this activity comes to an end, a new dawn begins within and we bless all things external.

We have lost the Divine Perspective and without it, we know nothing of,

I am under no laws but God's.

It thus remains intellectual and empty.

Shall we look into how it is that we have lost the Divine Perspective and have gotten caught in man-made rules?

There was a time when what you really are — your soul or spirit — was not separate from God. There was only Oneness. You were expressing it one way, someone else another way — creative like a happy dance and rhythm.

Everything in life that is alive extends what it is.

This is the Law of God not of any country. The sparrow gives birth to a sparrow, not to a cat.

The man who lives by the Laws of God, then, is independent and extends freedom no matter where he is. For freedom is something within one; it is not subject to anything external. Extend the essence of what you really are and no one can bind you.

If it has become clear that everything in creation extends itself, then I hope it has also become clear that this extending is the Law of God, and is creative. It is not isolated. Everything in creation contributes to make it work.

In man, all the planetary forces are focused. Therefore, when he becomes creative, he expresses the universe. He is not alone. Thus, he is grateful to everything because he is not separate from life, or anything of life. On the other hand, when you extend the rules of man, fear, war and hate come into being.

When you cease to live according to the Laws of God, you become tyrannical, no matter where you are. The more advantages you have, the worse it becomes. Humanity spends more money on armament than any other single commodity. Violence is promoted by television and magazines. Behold its extension: hate is for sale everywhere.

Wake up and see what manmade rules are extending, what nationalism is extending. Are they not all promoting the same fear, insecurity and unfulfillment?

I am under no laws but God's.

Who can say this as truth? How did we lose the Divine Perspective?

Let us continue. The Sons of God were the extensions of God, and therefore without form. A desire arose to perceive creation, but in order to perceive, a body was necessary. Having the same abilities as the Mind of God to extend and to create — those *are* our powers — we created a body, thus separating ourself from extension and limiting ourself to a form. From then, we began to extend body form to body form. And the Divine Perspective — the remembrance of the Spirit that we are — was forgotten.

In the beginning the bodies were subtle, more of light. They were not yet so bound and engrossed in time. But with the progression of time and its effects, spirit now bound to body became trapped in time and space. And for eons continued this way. This was the descent into matter.

But at any time, we can bring a different sensitivity within our bodies so that we are not bound to the body, but rather we use it as a vehicle — as you would use a pair of shoes.

Because we have identified with the body as our reality, our sense of identity has been lost. In earlier times, at least we identified ourselves with God. But now we are earthbound for the most part, identifying only with the body. And that is the "me."

The minute you become the "me," you live by the rules of external authority and control. And we do not know what to do. We have lost trust and faith in our God-created Self, that we can do what

God can do. Thus, we remain subject to the dilemma of jobs and survival.

> *Think of the freedom in the recognition that you are not bound by all the strange and twisted laws you have set up to save you. You really think that you would starve unless you have stacks of green paper strips and piles of metal discs. You really think a small round pellet or some fluid pushed into your veins through a sharpened needle will ward off disease and death. You really think you are alone unless another body is with you.*

> *It is insanity that thinks these things. You call them laws, and put them under different names in a long catalogue of rituals that have no use and serve no purpose. You think you must obey the "laws" of medicine, of economics and of health. Protect the body, and you will be saved.*

> *These are not laws, but madness.*[19]

The human brain pursues activity because it is afraid to know itself. To do so would mean dying to the "me," where the identification with the body ceases and the one with God begins.

> *There are no laws except the laws of God. This needs repeating, over and over, until you realize it applies to everything that you have made in opposition to God's Will. Your magic has no meaning. What it is meant to save does not exist. Only what it is meant to hide will save you.*

> *The laws of God can never be replaced.*[20]

The memory of who we are still exists. It is guarded by our Creator. But we do not want to go near it. To know our reality is the greatest dread in almost everyone today. We search and seek — making sure never to find it.

> *Think further; you believe in the "laws" of friendship, of "good" relationships and reciprocity. Perhaps you even think that there are laws which set forth what is God's and what is yours. Many "religions" have been based on this. They would not save but damn in Heaven's name. Yet they are no more strange that other "laws" you hold must be obeyed to make you safe.*
>
> *There are no laws but God's.*[21]

Caught in the extension of the brain — the body — we prevent the stillness that ensues from the discovery and the knowledge of who we are. Stillness is necessary and of this we are afraid. Our law has become fear.

Fear only came into existence when the illusion of separation of man from God began. Fear is not natural to man. Fear is not a Law of God. It is of your identification with the body.

Separation loves to learn about this as information. It loves preoccupation. It will seek, too, to come to God, but it will make sure never to find it. "To find it" is possible at this moment. Separation loves time and so it says, "It takes time, I need a technique, I need a guru." And we never question who is extending this need of a guru or of time?

The awareness that questions is of God. Awareness is our natural birthright. It needs no education, nor anything external to bring it about. The external can obscure the awareness by assuming authority over you. You give it the authority by thinking that you are helpless and incapable. We belittle ourselves constantly. We put ourselves in a position whereby we think someone else is superior.

Yet, Christ has said:

> ". . . He that believeth on me, the works that I do shall he do also; and greater works than these shall he do . . ."[22]

This is the Divine Perspective, free of time and space in which nothing is separated. It does not see appearances. It sees life as One.

The Law of God is not something imposed upon you. It is something that you are, that brings about perfection and creativity. It is the Law of Love. In Love, separation ends.

> ". . . forgive them;
> for they know not what they do."[23]

is a statement of Love's extension. In it there is no reaction. It recognizes you as the eternal being that you are. Wanting to sincerely see this as fact invokes in you the power of the Laws of God. Your integrity is your prayer and strength.

Find time in your life to come to an intensity of silence within you. For in the one who is content, the duality and the seeking have ended. For now he is not an extension of thought, but of Love.

Do not make yourself little. Know that you are blessed, for blessing is the Law of God and you are subject to no laws but His. All your needs will be met when you come to that honesty within yourself.

CHAPTER 25

Working With
A COURSE IN MIRACLES

"Today I Claim The Gifts Forgiveness Gives."

I will not wait another day to find the treasures that my Father offers me. Illusions are all vain, and dreams are gone even while they are woven out of thoughts that rest on false perceptions. Let me not accept such meager gifts again today. God's Voice is offering the peace of God to all who hear and choose to follow Him. This is my choice today. And so I go to find the treasures God has given me.[24]

THE FIRST ACTION would have to be confronting the brain with its knowings. *A Course In Miracles* tells us that there is the activity of the brain and there is the Mind. The Mind is universal; the Mind is One. You cannot enter the Mind of God as long as you have judgment and unforgiving thoughts about another person. Is your brain letting go of all judgments and opinions, of all knowings and non-forgiveness? If it is not, then we are not interested in the Mind. We are still with the values of the brain and personality. Whatever is of the brain is in conflict with the Mind of God. There must be some attachment, some comfort, some delirium that keeps us there.

To be with the Mind would require conviction. It would require responsibility. It would have the vitality to silence every other intrusion.

What are you going to do with your knowings? To be the Mind is to know the Knowledge of God. Therefore we have to let go of our knowings rather than asserting them.

We are tormented by our knowings which are always of the brain. Thus we live in limitation. Where there is limitation, there is nothing but conclusions. And I do not accept a conclusion as a truth. Why? Because it limits.

But you can rise from the brain level and be related with that which is the Mind — the Knowledge of God that sees all we know is real.

Nothing I see. . .means anything.[25]

This is a statement of the Mind.

This is a course in miracles. And it says that if you read the lesson correctly, you would have miracle after miracle. A miracle is when the brain touches upon the Mind. Every single sentence of the lesson has a miracle in it because it touches what is of the Mind and becomes limitless, infinite. Constantly there is the discovery and recognition of:

I am as God created me.[26]

Do you get this out of a lesson? Why don't you?

The Course states that we are preoccupied with

our brain which is programmed and conditioned. And to it we are conformed. See how the stamp of limitation is upon us. Each person is a prisoner of it — a prisoner of insanity.

And the Grace of God, the Thoughts of God come to say,

GOD'S VOICE IS CALLING YOU.

God's Voice is offering the peace of God to all who hear and choose to follow Him.[27]

Within that sentence is the power to overcome the brain chatter. It stops because you have become the Mind that is universal, that is All, that is total.

Are you interested in these miracles? If your interest remains in blaming or judging another, is it possible? How we have wasted ourselves in the prison of insanity, caught in our own petty-mindedness! We cannot hear the Call.

It is a course in miracles. It says that God's Voice is calling me and offering the peace of God.

Would you hear? If you hear it, then the brain becomes silent and you become the Mind, instantly. And it can be said: a miracle has taken place. Do you read the Course that way?

Once you have made that contact, something has gotten established. Then whatever the brain thinks, you can say it is unreal. At least you are not dominated by it anymore. You would not limit another nor yourself. You would be finished with your phraseology with which you have been indoctrinated. And that brings about a silence, does it not?

You do not come to silence by sitting in a corner with folded legs. You come to silence with the energy that has seen the false as the false. This that sees the false as the false is the Mind. The brain cannot see it. This that sees the false as the false silences the brain.

To come to that silence we must take on the responsibility to recognize that whatever the brain says is not true. Then see what happens.

But we make ourselves comfortable with having opinions and judgments about other people. And we *also* want to come to the Mind. How is it possible? Look at the contradictions in our life.

The lesson goes on to say:

I seek but the eternal.[28]

Do you seek but the eternal? That is the Mind. You seek things of time. You seek things of thought. And at the level of thinking with thought — no matter what you do — the unforgiveness, judgments and opinions are there. Because that is what the brain is! Then the nationalisms are there; conventional religions are there; it goes on and on.

The brain has no direct relationship with the Mind. It lives in its own prison. Do you not want to get out of that? The Light of awareness would always see what is of brain activity and start to dispel its conclusions and knowings.

And then we can say, yes, we have now seen the truth:

My meaningless thoughts
are showing me a meaningless world.[29]

The Mind is not meaningless and the brain is. It is the action of the Mind that transforms everything that is of the brain. And the brain fights and crucifies people who bring the Kingdom of God to earth. It is so stupid that it does not even know what is of God and what is of vested interest. It just knows to react. And all its judgments are foolish.

I seek but the eternal.

Can you be consistent with that? Why do you not take a stand to live by the eternal? That would be conviction. And you would be doing it but for yourself. When you come to that clarity, you will be extending what is of the Mind, what is eternal.

The lesson continues:

*For Your Son can be content
with nothing less than this.*[30]

Who do you think is the Son? It is YOU. Why do you accept less? And you have all the power of Heaven to help you.

Today I would behold my brother sinless.[31]

That is the attribute of the Mind of God. The attribute of the brain is not that. It is judgmental. When you become judgmental, you can see that you are caught by the brain. See the deception of it and say: "From this day forth I undertake not to deceive myself."

And right away, something in you undoes it. What are you doing? You are activating the forces of the Mind within you. And that is when the miracles take place.

Each lesson has these challenges.

Today I would behold my brother sinless.

Today. Do you take this as today's commitment, today's benediction? If not, could you say you are serious?

Today I would behold my brother sinless.

This is what you would be doing all day today. The minute you would find some contradiction in another, or some wrong in another, you correct it and a miracle takes place.

Today I claim the gifts forgiveness gives.

You are then receiving the gifts of forgiveness. The brain will always be negative because it knows no love. It knows only hate and fear, and without exception, every one of its thoughts needs forgiveness.

Can we read the Course that way? That every time you hold negative thoughts about someone else, you can say,

Today I claim the gifts forgiveness gives.

And right away, you overcome whatever you were thinking. It is when you forgive internally that a miracle takes place.

The brain is personal; it is physical; it is conditioned. All it knows — basically, profoundly — is fear. And it has built its existence in separation rather than love. And in this conditioned brain we are caught.

The greatest gift of all is *A Course In Miracles* that

says: I can unite your brain with the Mind. It shows you that the brain is unreal and frees you from it. Every time a miracle takes place, you receive the Peace of God.

God's Voice is offering the peace of God. . .

It will lift you to be with the Peace of God. You become less and less dependent on the external and more and more with joy and gladness because these are the things that are eternal. The Peace of God is not a sensation.

Unless we undertake to live the Course, to bring it to application, we will not know the miracles. Each day there is a jewel the Course offers.

God's Voice is offering the peace of God
to all who hear and choose to follow Him.

There must be a tremendous appreciation for the gift of *A Course In Miracles* that frees man from his brain preoccupation. We are amongst those who have received it. What a blessing are the Thoughts of God! You are not of the world any longer. Some nobleness, something supreme and sublime has entered into you, for you have come to something like a total rebirth with the light of love in your heart. And you will see the world differently.

Your conflicts end because seeing the falseness of conflict is of the Mind. A miracle has taken place. You are no longer subservient to conflict, to desire, to knowings, to pressures, to fear. These are the basis of thought. And now you question it all.

It is such a vast action. It is not limited because nothing is outside of that Mind. When the action of the Mind takes place in you, you then affect every mind in the world. It is always the one person that has revolutionized everything. That One Mind ignites other minds. That Mind knows no helplessness. It knows no limitations.

You activate your Mind to stop the activity of the brain. Your Mind then can be a strength to all those who are caught by the brain. In the One Mind there is no separation. That Mind is you. And you can silence all the brain activity of another. You make miracles possible and you become a miracle worker.

God's Voice is offering the peace of God
to all who hear and choose to follow Him.

You will not longer follow the brain; you will not follow nationalisms, nor any other "ism." You follow what is of God, for that is what you extend.

Are you going to have the time to have that love relationship with the Course, that reverence for the Course? If brain activity is more important than taking on the commitment for the day, then know that you are not serious. That too would bring about a miracle. Anything that is true brings about a miracle. That is the beauty of it.

Would you then accept what the brain is saying? Not if you are earnest. There is no need to. It degrades one.

Know that it takes but an instant to vanish the world.

Only an instant does this world endure.[32]

Only an instant. . .

And the Course makes it possible. If you read the Course with reverence, nothing can endure that is of the brain, for the Son of God is not limited. Truth is not limited. Love is not limited. Only the chatter of the brain is limited, and the limited cannot rule what is not limited. The false cannot assume the authority of that which is real. There is nothing the brain offers that takes more than an instant for the Course to dissolve.

Miracles are at your command.

God's Plan for Salvation is for those who beyond all else see the urgency of being liberated. It takes but an instant to vanish the world. Whenever the world is trying to get hold of you, stop for a moment and see what the brain is doing. It is not of the Mind of God. It is separated. It lacks love; it has its fear. And you will value God's Plan for Salvation. They are not just words. They are a truth. And the light of that truth is the Course.

Having silenced the brain, you will discover that that was the action of the Mind freeing the Son of God from the web of illusions.

The brain knows no freedom from wanting. It always wants because it has no satisfaction and the ultimate wanting is being comfortable. That is where man's quest usually ends. The knowing of one truth shakes one up!

Every day there is a gift given and when you undertake:

Today I would behold my brother sinless.

you become a co-creator with it. The brain would make its mistakes but you would catch yourself. The awareness would come. The miracles would happen. Then nothing external can take you over, for you see that you are eternal.

Come to some honesty. If to be liberated is your intent, then you would not move toward that which binds you. You would have enough time to be silent, to bring things to order in order to extend that which is of the Mind of God.

There is an urgency. Find out if you are seeking comfort. That is all the brain can seek. Even when it says it wants liberation, it is a lie. Find out what the deceptions are. Discover:

> *My meaningless thoughts*
> *are showing me a meaningless world.*[33]

That is all they can see because thoughts are physical.

But the Mind is a light and a seeing that is direct. It sees only the holiness of God and the glory of creation. Even at the level of nature, see the glory of it, the order of it. The rain, the spring, the sun, the moon, the dawn, the day, the river, the birds, the seeds — leave one speechless. Have you ever seen from the state that is still?

To see deception one has to come to the Present. The thought system of the brain always introduces postponement and time. Thought itself is contradiction. That is where the trouble lies.

How we have found comfort in deception! How we have found comfort in illusion!

The consistency in *A Course In Miracles* says that every lesson imparts communication with the Divine. Within every lesson that must take place. We have to be consistent with that so that the action of the Mind can enter into the brain.

The Course says that every day, with every lesson, it is going to introduce us to that which is timeless. And so we have to be consistent with the Course. What is real is liberation. Everyday we can experience these miracles. Miracles are corrections — seeing the false as the false whereby we cannot be deceived anymore. That can happen today and it can happen every day.

The help is guaranteed in each lesson to come into contact with the Mind of God. It is the offer of Co-Creationship, a cooperation with the forces of the Mind of God that come to the brain level to lift it to that. How can we then lose out on what is of today?

If it does not take place now it will not take place later either. And something precious is being wasted. We are making time real because we are not with what is eternal, always here and now.

Every miracle is a liberation from brain activity, from illusion.

Religion means to never be deceived.
Let us put an end to deception.
A Course In Miracles is God's gift
to His beloved Son,
and it will never fail.

CHAPTER 26

Working With
A COURSE IN MIRACLES

"Peace To My Mind. Let All My Thoughts Be Still."

CAN WE MEET to know that which is not of words? Can we meet to dissolve the words? That would mean that we are no longer attached to ideas, that we have overcome the defending of ideas and want to go beyond them.

Begin to see what ideas are doing to humanity. All wars are based on them. Human life becomes secondary and the idea more important; ill-will for the opposite is justified and then we can *talk* about peace. How we love the limitation of ideas and not the limitless beings that we are.

Are you interested in discovering the limitlessness of your being? How would you fit into society when all over the world, the Reality of man is almost totally forgotten? What is it that we remember most? Is it not always some form of self-centeredness, some money-making endeavor that is important? How status-conscious we have become!

Have you ever felt the need of wisdom? That

you would like to talk with someone who is beyond ideas, whose voice extends the Word of God? Our ears cannot hear because we hear the voice of our own interpretations.

The man who extends the Word of God does hear and is affected by the Word. For truth is very expansive. It is the light of the world. The trees can respond to it but the human being is deaf with his own interpretation.

And Lesson 221 of *A Course In Miracles* says:

Peace to my mind. Let all my thoughts be still.[34]

If you and I cannot come to *Peace to my mind*, then what good is our learning? If the mind cannot know peace, what good is all the working and the struggle, the life of routine and drudgery?

Let all my thoughts be still.

Until and unless we are still, we will not hear the Word of God. We will only hear words and ideas. Ideas we can like or dislike but they are not true. What is true goes beyond agreement and disagreement, beyond armament and artificiality.

A mind at peace is free from ideas. It has wisdom — wisdom to be free of all that is external. The man who knows:

Peace to my mind. Let all my thoughts be still.

would be one who does not seek to achieve or accomplish anything external.

If you ask, ''How would he survive?'' can you see that your life is given to survival?

Could one dare question, go deeply into something? Discover that if you do not want to accomplish or achieve anything externally, you must be at peace. You must have the resources of stillness, of which we as yet know very little.

Stillness is of the Kingdom of God. Ideas are earth-born. The one who is still receives that which is of Heaven.

> "Thy Kingdom come.
> Thy will be done in earth,
> as it is in heaven."[35]

There are great beings who never make a cause of anything. Never try to *save the world*. That "doing" is the biggest play of the ego. A person who can contain himself leaves a greater blessing upon the earth.

But we value activity. And activity is always promoted by ideas. It has nothing to do with stillness and peace. And we know nothing other than activity. We judge another person by his activity. "He is a vice-president." Or, "He owns a restaurant." We worship activity.

The action of Love is born out of fulfillment. It cannot be personal. Activity is of self-centeredness. It is the action of ambition. Yet we are children of Love.

Anyone who can say:

Peace to my mind. Let all my thoughts be still.

can receive what is of the Grace of God and put It into action. They are free of ideas and they are inspired. Always it is the action of Love and not the activity of intellectual ideas.

Do we know the difference? Have we ever known anyone who is the action of Love? Can you name one person you know who is the action of the Universe, the action of the Spirit, the extension of God's Will, who never indulges in the activity of ideas? We are trained for the activity of ideas. That is our education.

Peace to my mind.

Can we hear these words? By hearing, I mean to know the truth.

If you do not mentalize it, if you do not interpret it, if you do not have ideas — you are better off. Can you afford to let go of your ideas? Can you trust? Could you say to yourself:

Let all my thoughts be still?

Will they be still? And if they are not still, then know you are listening to your own inner chatter.

Words that are not of ideas have the power to bring the mind to peace and all thoughts to stillness. What we need is peace and stillness, not more ideas. Peace and stillness would impart wisdom to us. And in stillness, you and I would find what our real function is.

The function may have nothing to do with a job. No man who is of God can do another's work. For his own work is related to what is eternal.

Thus we bring to this time level that which is of eternity and our life is blessed. We have to come to,

"Love ye one another." We are at peace for doing something that is boundless. It introduces us to our own limitlessness, and we are free. We no longer get into the mortal fuss. We see human beings as children of God and not as Mexicans or Canadians, Moslems or Hindus, capitalists or socialists. If we are caught in our limitations, then prejudice blinds our vision.

You have a responsibility to discover your own holiness. Each person must discover:

Peace to my mind. Let all my thoughts be still.

and come to the state of the prayer:

Father, I come to You today to seek the peace that You alone can give. I come in silence. In the quiet of my heart, the deep recesses of my mind, I wait and listen for Your Voice. My Father, speak to me today. I come to hear Your Voice in silence and in certainty and love, sure You will hear my call and answer me.[36]

Within this prayer is a Divine vibration to introduce one to the actuality of that state.

Therefore the lesson is not an idea. We cannot read the Course as if it were *Reader's Digest*. We have to put our hearts into it, put our love into it. Go to the Course with reverence. Go to it with quiet. Then read with the boundless space. It is the space you and I give to it that would make it flower.

You read in order to receive this state and not in order to have an idea *about* it. Would you not rather have the state than the idea? Can one really say, as though speaking to our Creator:

Father, I come to You today
to seek the peace that You alone can give.

Do you really believe that? If you do not, then why say it? Discover that you are partial. You believe it, and then you do not believe it. A half-way thing will not work.

It requires wholeheartedness for it to be a prayer. If you are totally with it, it is answered. Then you will have no doubt in your mind that it will be met. As long as it is partial, there is always going to be some lingering doubt. And the doubt defeats it.

Once a prayer is uttered, it is answered beyond all expectations, for you sense the boundlessness of yourself. You would be too wise and too much at peace to be demonstrative, or even touched by need, for you would be liberated. There is only One Mind. And when you are in that State, you have the potentials of God. Real prayer liberates man and brings him to the discovery:

I am not a body. I am free.
For I am still as God created me. [37]

You have to receive with a mind that is open and still, full of reverence. And if the chatter of thought goes on, let it be. As long as *you* do not give it energy, it will subside.

Father, I come to You today
to seek the peace that You alone can give.
I come in silence.

If you are not in silence, then you have not

come. Every sentence, every word tells us: Listen.
Make yourself silent.

> *I come in silence.*
> *In the quiet of my heart,*
> *the deep recesses of my mind,*
> *I wait and listen to Your Voice.*

What a preparation to receive!

> *My Father, speak to me today.*
> *I come to hear Your Voice*
> *in silence and certainty . . .*

You cannot come to silence until you are certain.
Discover these things. They are jewels. Without
certainty there is no silence.

> *. . . in silence and in certainty and love,*
> *sure You will hear my call and answer me.*

These are the words of Christ. Listen to them.

> *Now do we wait in quiet.*
> *God is here. . .*[38]

He is with you because you wait together.

> *I am sure that He will speak to you, and you*
> *will hear. Accept my confidence, for it is yours.*
> *Our minds are joined. We wait with one intent;*
> *to hear our Father's answer to our call, to let*
> *our thoughts be still and find His peace, to hear*
> *Him speak to us of what we are, and to reveal*
> *Himself unto His Son.*[39]

Real prayer is to want nothing other than to
know who you are. Once you know who you are,
you know what holiness is. And everything in

nature exists to bring you to that perfection.

Let all my thoughts be still.

The ideas are gone, and love and stillness and certainty are there. Certainty knows to love another. It does not make you dependent.

The Course assures us:

Nothing real can be threatened.
Nothing unreal exists.[40]

Bring to your remembrance what it is — your own Reality. This remembrance means you are declaring your freedom from time and external pressures because you dare to remember that you are eternal.

Just as night brings its shelter
the light of the day brings its blessing.
Live with peace in your heart,
value stillness and know
you are loved by God.
This is the truth.

There is no love in personality's world, but we are loved by God. Once we know that as truth, we can love all of mankind and honor what Christ has said, "LOVE YE ONE ANOTHER."

Love remains Love. It never turns bitter or hateful. If it does it is not Love. Love knows no judgment. Love is your own richness that no one can take away.

Peace to my mind.
Let all my thoughts be still.

Part 7

The Last Judgment

Peace be to you. There is no instant when
You stand alone; no time when God will fail
To take your hand; no moment when His Love
Does not surround you, comfort you and care,
Along with you, for every wish you have,
Each little joy or tiny stab of pain.
At one with you forever, He remains
Your one relationship; your only Friend.
You are the holy Son of God Himself.
Peace be to you, for what is His is yours.[1]

CHAPTER 27

Assurances Of Christ
"You Do Not Walk Alone"[2]

Y OU ARE THE *work of God, and His work is wholly lovable and wholly loving. This is how a man must think of himself in his heart, because this is what he is.*[3]

> *I assure you that I will witness for anyone who lets me, and to whatever extent he permits it.*[4]

Child of God, you were created to create the good, the beautiful and the holy. Do not forget this.[5]

> *God is lonely without His Sons, and they are lonely without Him.*[6]

When everything you retain is lovable, there is no reason for fear to remain with you. This is your part in the Atonement.[7]

> *Nothing can prevail against a Son of God who commends his Spirit into the Hands of his Father.*[8]

If you are willing to renounce the role of guardian of your thought system and open it to me, I will correct it very gently and lead you back to God.[9]

> *When you are afraid, be still and know that God is real, and you are His beloved Son in whom He is well pleased.*[10]

I will teach with you and live with you if you will think with me. . .[11]

> *Let us ask the Father in my name to keep you mindful of His Love for you and yours for Him. He has never failed to answer this request. . . . Those who call truly are always answered.*[12]

As a loving brother I am deeply concerned with your mind, and urge you to follow my example as you look at yourself and at your brother, and see in both the glorious creations of a glorious Father.[13]

> *My trust in you is greater than yours in me at the moment, but it will not always be that way. Your mission is very simple. You are asked to live so as to demonstrate that you are not an ego, and I do not choose God's channels wrongly. My chosen channels cannot fail, because I will lend them my strength as long as theirs is wanting.*[14]

. . .unless you take part in the creation, His joy is not complete because yours is incomplete. And this He does know. He knows it in His Own Being and its experience of His Son's experience.

*The constant going out of His Love is blocked
when His channels are closed, and He is lonely
when the minds He created do not communicate
fully with Him.* [15]

> *What we can accomplish together has no limits,
> because the Call for God is the call to the unlimit-
> ed. Child of God, my message is for you, to hear
> and give away as you answer the Holy Spirit
> within you.* [16]

*You can indeed depart in peace because I have
loved you as I loved myself. You go with my blessing and for my blessing. Hold it and share it, that
it may always be ours. I place the peace of God in
your heart and in your hands, to hold and share.
The heart is pure to hold it, and the hands are
strong to give it. We cannot lose. My judgment is
as strong as the wisdom of God, in Whose Heart
and Hands we have our being. His quiet children
are His blessed Sons. The Thoughts of God are
with you.* [17]

> *You are a child of God, a priceless part of His
> Kingdom, which He created as part of Him.
> Nothing else exists and only this is real.* [18]

*When I said "I am with you always," I meant it
literally. I am not absent to anyone in any situation. Because I am always with you, you are the
way, the truth and the life.* [19]

> *The certain are perfectly calm, because they are
> not in doubt. They do not raise questions, because*

nothing questionable enters their minds. This holds them in perfect serenity, because this is what they share, knowing what they are.[20]

Keep His way to remember yourself, and teach His way lest you forget yourself. Give only honor to the Sons of the living God, and count yourself among them gladly.[21]

> *I go before you because I am beyond the ego. Reach, therefore, for my hand because you want to transcend the ego. My strength will never be wanting, and if you choose to share it you will do so. I give it willingly and gladly, because I need you as much as you need me.*[22]

God is Love and you do want Him. This is your will. Ask for this and you will be answered. . . because you will be asking only for what belongs to you.[23]

> *My brother, you are part of God and part of me. . . . I come to you from our Father to offer you everything again. . . . I give you the lamp and I will go with you. You will not take this journey alone. I will lead you to your true Father, Who hath need of you, as I have. Will you not answer the call of love with joy?*[24]

O my child, if you knew what God wills for you, your joy would be complete! And what He wills has happened, for it was always true. When the light comes and you have said, ''God's Will is mine,'' you will see such beauty that you will know it is not of you. Out of your joy you will

*create beauty in His Name, for your joy could no
more be contained than His. The bleak little world
will vanish into nothingness, and your heart will
be so filled with joy that it will leap into Heaven,
and into the Presence of God.* [25]

*. . .love yourself with the Love of Christ, for so
does your Father love you. You can refuse to
enter, but you cannot bar the door that Christ
holds open. Come unto me who holds it open for
you, for while I live it cannot be shut, and I live
forever. God is my life and yours, and nothing is
denied by God to His Son.* [26]

*Blessed are you who are willing to ask the truth of
God without fear, for only thus can you learn
that His answer is the release from fear. Beautiful
child of God, you are asking only for what I
promised you. Do you believe I would deceive
you?* [27]

*Love him who is beloved of his Father, and you
will learn of the Father's Love for you.* [28]

*A little while and you will see me. . . . Trust in my
help, for I did not walk alone, and I will walk
with you as our Father walked with me.* [29]

*And as your hymns of praise and gladness rise to
your Creator, He will return your thanks in His
clear Answer to your call. For it can never be that
His Son called upon Him and remained unan-
swered. His call to you is but your call to Him.
And in Him you are answered by His peace.* [30]

255

. . .I treasure you beyond the value that you set on yourself, even unto the worth that God has placed upon you. I love all that He created, and all my faith and my belief I offer unto it. My faith in you is as strong as all the love I give my Father. My trust in you is without limit, and without the fear that you will hear me not. I thank the Father for your loveliness. . . . [31]

See only praise of Him in what He has created, for He will never cease His praise of you. United in this praise we stand before the gates of Heaven where we will surely enter in our sinlessness. God loves you. [32]

Have faith in only this one thing, and it will be sufficient: God wills you be in Heaven, and nothing can keep you from it, or it from you. [33]

Offer your faith to Me, and I will place it gently in the holy place where it belongs. You will find no deception there, but only the simple truth. And you will love it because you will understand it. [34]

Whenever you are in doubt what you should do, think of His Presence in you, and tell yourself this, and only this:

> *"He leadeth me and knows the way,
> which I know not.
> Yet He will never keep from me
> what He would have me learn.
> And so I trust Him to communicate to me
> all that He knows for me."* [35]

*Blessed are you who teach with me. Our power
comes not from us, but of our Father.*[36]

*The Atonement is so gentle you need but whisper
to it, and all its power will rush to your assistance
and support. You are not frail with God beside
you.*[37]

*Leave room for Him, and you will find yourself so
filled with power that nothing will prevail
against your peace. And this will be the test by
which you recognize that you have understood.*[38]

*Holy Child of God, when will you learn that only
holiness can content you and give you peace?*[39]

*For God will take the last step swiftly, when you
have reached the real world and have been made
ready for Him.*[40]

*If you knew Who walks beside you on the way
that you have chosen, fear would be impossible.*[41]

*. . . I stand with you and walk with you in your
advance to truth. And where we go we carry God
with us.*[42]

*Salvation flows from deep within the home you
offered to my Father and to me. And we are there
together, in the quiet communion in which the
Father and the Son are joined. O come ye faithful
to the holy union of the Father and the Son in
you!*[43]

And let us join in faith that He Who brought us here together will offer you the innocence you need, and that you will accept it for my love and His.[44]

> *Behold your Friend, the Christ Who stands beside you. How holy and beautiful He is!*[45]

Together we will disappear into the Presence beyond the veil, not to be lost but found; not to be seen but known. And knowing, nothing in the plan God has established for salvation will be left undone.[46]

> *Nothing you need will be denied you. Not one seeming difficulty but will melt away before you reach it. You need take thought for nothing, careless of everything except the only purpose that you would fulfill. As that was given you, so will its fulfillment be. God's guarantee will hold against all obstacles, for it rests on certainty and not contingency. It rests on you. And what can be more certain than a Son of God?*[47]

Be comforted, and feel the Holy Spirit watching over you in love and perfect confidence in what He sees.[48]

> *Love's arms are open to receive you, and give you peace forever.*[49]

Little child, innocent of sin, follow in gladness the way to certainty. Be not held back by fear's insane insistence that sureness lies in doubt. This

*has no meaning. The quiet way is open. Follow it
happily, and question not what must be so.* [50]

*You are your brother's savior. He is yours. Rea-
son speaks happily indeed of this. This gracious
plan was given love by Love. And what Love
plans is like Itself in this: Being united, It would
have you learn what you must be. And being one
with It, it must be given you to give what It has
given, and gives still. Spend but an instant in the
glad acceptance of what is given you to give your
brother, and learn with him what has been given
both of you. To give is no more blessed than to
receive. But neither is it less.* [51]

*Think of the loveliness that you will see, who
walk with Him! And think how beautiful will
each of you look to the other!* [52]

*God rests with you in quiet, undefended and whol-
ly undefending, for in this quiet state alone is
strength and power.* [53]

*Child of peace, the light has come to you. The
light you bring you do not recognize, and yet you
will remember. Who can deny himself the vision
that he brings to others? And who would fail to
recognize a gift he let be laid in Heaven through
himself? The gentle service that you give the Holy
Spirit is service to yourself. You who are now His
means must love all that He loves. And what you
bring is your remembrance of everything that is
eternal. No trace of anything in time can long
remain in minds that serve the timeless. And no*

illusion can disturb the peace of a relationship that has become the means of peace.[54]

   He [God] loves you perfectly, completely and eternally.[55]

You who are beloved of Him are no illusion, being as true and holy as Himself. The stillness of your certainty of Him and of yourself is home to both of You, Who dwell as one and not apart.[56]

   How can you know whether you chose the stairs to Heaven or the way to hell? Quite easily. How do you feel? Is peace in your awareness? Are you certain which way you go? And are you sure the goal of Heaven can be reached? If not, you walk alone. Ask, then, your Friend to join with you, and give you certainty of where you go.[57]

The Christ in you is very still. He looks on what He loves, and knows it as Himself. And thus does He rejoice at what He sees, because He knows that it is one with Him and with His Father.[58]

   How little is the hindrance that withholds the wealth of Heaven from you. And how great will be the joy in Heaven when you join the mighty chorus to the Love of God![59]

Without Him you are friendless. Seek not another friend to take His place. There is no other friend.[60]

*Around you angels hover lovingly, to keep away
all darkened thoughts of sin, and keep the light
where it has entered in.* [61]

*Be not afraid of blessing, for the One Who blesses
you loves all the world, and leaves nothing
within the world that could be feared.* [62]

> *God keeps His promises; His Son keeps his. In his
> creation did his Father say, ''You are beloved of
> Me and I of you forever. Be you perfect as Myself,
> for you can never be apart from Me.''* [63]

Your Guest has *come. You asked Him, and He
came. You did not hear Him enter, for you did not
wholly welcome Him. And yet His gifts came
with Him. He has laid them at your feet, and asks
you now that you will look on them and take
them for your own.* [64]

> *How holy are you, that the Son of God can be
> your savior in the midst of dreams of desolation
> and disaster.* [65]

*The Son of Life cannot be killed. He is immortal as
his Father. What he is cannot be changed. He is
the only thing in all the universe that must be
one.* [66]

> *Let Him remind you of His Love for you, and do
> not seek to drown His Voice in chants of deep
> despair to idols of yourself. Seek not outside your
> Father for your hope. For hope of happiness is
> not despair.* [67]

*The star still shines; the sky has never changed.
But you, the holy Son of God Himself, are unaware of your reality.*[68]

> *How light and easy is the step across the narrow
> boundaries of the world of fear where you have
> recognized Whose Hand you hold!. . . For He
> Whose hand you hold was waiting but for you to
> join Him.*[69]

*The Christ in you remembers God with all the
certainty with which He knows His Love.*[70]

> *Christ calls to all with equal tenderness, seeing
> no leaders and no followers, and hearing but one
> answer to them all. Because He hears one Voice,
> he cannot hear a different answer from the one He
> gave when God appointed Him His only Son.*[71]

*For next to you is One Who holds the light before
you, so that every step is made in certainty and
sureness of the road . . . . And He Who travels
with you* has *the light.*[72]

> *Your will be done, you holy child of God. It does
> not matter if you think you are in earth or
> Heaven. What your Father wills of you can never
> change. The truth in you remains as radiant as a
> star, as pure as light, as innocent as love itself.
> And you* are *worthy that your will be done!*[73]

*Deny me not the little gift I ask, when in ex-
change I lay before your feet the peace of God, and
power to bring this peace to everyone who*

wanders in the world uncertain, lonely, and in constant fear. For it is given you to join with him, and through the Christ in you unveil his eyes, and let him look upon the Christ in him.[74]

Addenda

Autobiography Of Tara Singh

TARA SINGH, the teacher of the School at *The Branching of the Road,*[1] spent his early years in the village of Punjab, India.

"I came from a background in India of living in a spacious house with one door, where my parents and grandparents, sister, uncles, aunts, cousins and nephews lived together. The one door signifies that our house was not divided and for centuries we had lived in harmony. Wisdom resided there and lifted us out of irritation and reaction. The elders extended goodness and we grew up surrounded with affection and a sense of reverence for life. No one in the family had ever been career oriented. We had agricultural land and were an honored family. We considered ourselves affluent. The one door stood as the symbol of unity.

"The family was religious and even

without knowing it, I absorbed the values of the spirit. Some of us extended ourselves beyond the village and beyond the boundaries of self-centeredness.

''During my formative years, there was an innate resistance to imposed, formal education. I sensed that it was not right and felt false submitting to it. It was so much inferior to what one learned directly. *That* I enjoyed and the imposed appeared harmful. The teacher even had to resort to tying me to a tree during the six months that I attended school because I repeatedly ran away to play in the fields or by the village pond. All my life, however, I learned through what awakened my interest. And I later discovered that natural intelligence is autonomous; it can cope with anything and has its own capacity to learn.''

From this sheltered environment, at the age of nine, Tara Singh and his mother and uncles traveled to Panama via Europe to join his father who was in business there. While in Panama he attended school for two years. At the age of eighteen, he and his mother returned to India and he found himself caught in a conspiracy to get him married. Inspired by the family saint, at the age of twenty-one, his search for Truth and God led him to the Himalayas.

''For four years, I wholeheartedly applied myself to a religious life of devotion and discipline. I had flashes of insight that led me to question and to undo my own knowing. I realized that Truth is independent of time and conventional religion, and a mind conditioned by religious or secular beliefs is always limited. I emerged from the solitary years with discrimination and the capacity to receive and to heed. Disillusionment brought about a sudden change of value, but to be freed from the mask of pious attitude and to outgrow tradition is an invaluable experience. Now I insisted upon being responsible, on questioning and coming to clarity before getting involved."

In his next phase of growth, Tara Singh responded to the poverty of India through participation in that country's postwar industrialization. The great beings he met were his best teachers. He was forever affected by how wisely they lived and the goodness they shared.

"There were several wise men of intrinsic life and consistent knowledge who made a strong impact on my life. One of the most extraordinary men was Giani Kartar Singh. I met him on a train at Amritsar on the way to Lahore in 1945. He came and sat opposite me in the compartment. I was in crisis, burning to make contact and not knowing how to approach him. But the energy of first thought acts involuntarily. Gianiji, an eminent man, was the saintly, genius leader of the Sikhs. His Sikhism encompassed all humanity in its range; his nationalism was unlimited humanism.

''This contact opened totally new dimensions and potentials within me and made things possible in an India besieged by the cruelty of poverty. It culminated in an enormous industrial project at the grass roots level and capital of over six million dollars supported by Sikhs, Maharajahs, and others, but most of all by Gianiji's impeccable integrity.

''He was a man of renunciation and religious outlook who never had a bank account. The force of his love transformed my life and in his atmosphere, I blossomed. He offered an intimate relationship through which I became a friend of Prime Minister Nehru and other eminent leaders of incorruptible lives. He had said when people asked him, 'What do you see in Tara Singh?'

'The word ''impossible'' does not apply to him. He will not accept second best and this will make him or break him.'

''In 1947, the advent of freedom and the partition of India and Pakistan disrupted the humanistic plan. I was virtually penniless and homeless but felt the need to visit the West and make an individual survey of the impact of science on society before embarking upon another venture. One questioned what part the gigantic, underdeveloped, agrarian society of almost two billion was to play in the Post War period. Would the West heed India's authentic voice — the wisdom of its unbiased outlook — and avert the spread of tension? The media was accelerating Cold War propaganda, and nationalism was being drummed into the collective consciousness.''

It was in the 1950's, discovering that man's problems cannot be solved externally, that Mr. Singh was inspired by his association with Mr. J. Krishnamurti.

''At the end of 1947, soon after the independence of India, I arrived in England and then came to New York to meet with those at an international level who made decisions and determined human destiny. In the West, I met a great many men and women of excellence. Very quickly I came into contact with the mind of the age and found there was little use for wisdom which never makes survival its first concern. Skills had become important and man was rapidly losing his work and becoming subject to jobs. I was startled by the power of the media with its ability to influence collective consciousness, the panic about communism, and the stimulated daily life obsessed with problems. These were just facts, not good or bad, but what was.

''The background of the Sikh religion prior to meeting Gianiji was essential to the new awakening. Similarly, before meeting with Mr. J. Krishnamurti, it was essential to be aware of world affairs. For me the cultural life of New York City revolved around the work of the United Nations and various philanthropic organizations. I was captivated by the creative spirit of the West. New York at the time seemed like the capital of the world and I was overwhelmed by the music, art, theatre and literature which it offered. Also, contact with the lofty voices of the forefathers of the New World — Emerson, Thoreau, Whitman, and Lincoln — enriched my life.

''It was in New York that I literally learned to read. Loneliness compelled me to it. Usually the hours spent reading from 8:00 p.m. to 2:00 a.m. became the most rewarding time in my life and this continued for years irrespective of where I lived in the world.

''To outgrow is always blessed — not to get stuck, but to be enriched by the deeper expression of life on the planet. It was a good background to meet with Mr. Krishnamurti and enter the realm of eternal laws.

''It was on my second trip to America in 1953, that I met Mr. J. Krishnamurti in New York. In twenty minutes, all that I knew or pretended to know, or wished to do, disappeared. The contact was so strong it put an end to the bondage of my knowing and lifted me to what is not of words. Never could I have conceived the blessing of such a sacred encounter. I remember thinking to myself as I walked through Central Park that it was a blessing to be born at the time that such a great being was upon the planet. The unchangeable light of his word extended itself and still continues to expand its newness in me.

"A few years later, I arrived in Ojai, California, a week before the annual 'Talks' began and met with Mr. Krishnamurti daily. When I attended his first 'Talk' at the end of that week, he looked at everyone in the audience prior to beginning to speak, as was his custom. When his eyes met mine for a fleeting instant, it imparted a joy, a tremendous blessing, and I was given the ears to hear.[2] After the 'Talk' I sat for hours transfixed.

"The next day, when I met with him, I told him that I understood what he had shared beyond the words. We sat in silence a while and then he said:

> 'Drop everything.
> Be still.
> The seeds are sown,
> leave it alone.'

"It took years for me to know the full significance of his words. Year after year, I continued to discover what 'the seeds are sown' meant and the responsibility that Mr. Krishnamurti assumed. The God-lit Teacher imparts the energy that brings one to stillness and the gratefulness out of which the next action emerges. He guarded me directly, and indirectly, from ever getting involved in what was not part of creation — in the end to extend the True Knowledge of eternal seeds with which he blessed me. The energy of gratefulness then enabled me to relate with what is eternal.

"The only true relationship is between the Teacher and the student. It is not between parents and children, nor between wives and husbands. All these fall short of timelessness. It is the relationship with the Teacher that ends the separation and brings one to the Oneness of Life and the One Mind of God. The relationship is eternal and does not end in death. Its action continues as the student harnesses the energy of joyous responsibility and realizes that that which is real emerges out of his own stillness and gratefulness. From 1953, meetings with Mr. Krishnamurti continued now and then. I was not a regular devotee, but he remained my constant companion in life.

"In 1963, I brought all loose ends to a head and had even outgrown wanting to help the world. I had been involved in world affairs, increasing the per capita income of underdeveloped areas. Through this work I realized:

> Times will reveal themselves — that you cannot depend on the externals. Without the externals, there is no personality and there is no relationship at the personality level. The fear of the externals will destroy the manmade, external world.

"I felt the spaciousness of noninvolvement with either person, place or activity and went to Switzerland to attend Mr. Krishnamurti's 'Talks.' In the winter of 1963, I had an interview with Mr. Krishnamurti in Madras. I said that I had come to give myself totally to a life of the spirit. He startled me by saying: 'Go and earn some money.' But I said, 'Sir, I have made up my mind. I do not want to live the life of the world. It has no fascination for me.' He stopped me short and repeated what he had said before, 'Go and earn some money.'

"I was under the impression that a sannyasi who lived a vertical life did not touch money. The tradition in India was established that men and women of renunciation were fed by the householder. I pleaded my seriousness. Mr. Krishnamurti said, 'Go and earn some money or I will never see you again.' This time, the *or else* gave me no option but to heed. Instantly the duality ended and my own heeding transmitted a sense of joy so energetic its profound meaning still continues to unfold.

His words, when heeded, are those that have no ending.
They light the passage of your life.

"I had only about $20 in all to my name when I started. As I was leaving, an additional instruction was given by Mr. Krishnamurti: 'Do not ever take advantage of another.'

"How difficult it is to end the preference for advantages. One wants to lead a spiritual life, but could this ever be within our present thought system based on motives?

"The words of Mr. Krishnamurti, who was free of personality, and like Jesus and Lord Buddha owned nothing, ordain an action in one that contains the vitality to actualize its completion. This discovery is the blessing. I learned that the action of Life is impersonal; activity is devoid of action. My whole mind gathered itself to earning money and within four months I had acquired sixty thousand dollars.

"In this age, it is difficult to lead a truly religious life without one's own independent means. Without money, one invariably resorts to exploitation and ends up needing people for one's own projects.

"The responsibility for the right use of
money was the next step. What wisdom it
would take to make right use of a dollar.

I will not value what is valueless.[3]

"What discrimination it takes to end
wastage, deny yourself nothing, nor look
at price tags, but be with the essential
always."

Subsequently, Tara Singh became more and
more removed from worldly affairs and devoted
several years of his life to the study and the practice
of Raja Yoga and the non-commercial lifestyle of
the enlightened beings of the Vedas and the Upanishads. During this time he also came into close
contact with the teachings of Sri Ramakrishna and
Sri Ramana Maharshi. The discipline imparted
through Raja Yoga helped make possible a three
year period of silent retreat.

"Mr. Krishnamurti warned me that
Hatha Yoga is merely physical and stressed
the importance of health and discipline in
life. The deeper meaning of discipline that
is not imposed but has its own order began
to reveal itself. It awakened a passion that
had no alternatives. This led me to spend
three years in silence in Carmel, California.

"Silence, ever whole, has its own wisdom of non-dependence and succeeds
effortlessly in coping with all the essen-
tials without the need of another. It has its
own independent existence. Not imposed

from without, it is of an inner yearning to be with the spacious aloneness in which one is related to all that is. Silence is not isolation seeking some projected goal of self-improvement.

"As I emerged from silence, I saw that hardly anyone listens and realized why Jesus placed so much emphasis on '. . . having the ears to hear.' Without it, one cannot communicate. Learning is abstract; it is of things and ideas that have names; it is deceptive for it is based on interpretation. But to communicate and to heed demands an attentive, receptive, and silent mind. Self honesty or truth requires consistency at all levels of one's being.

"Inwardly, there arose a yearning in me to be productive. True productivity is not projected but is independent of the externals. It is without direction. It can only be the extension of the Divine Will, the only Reality."

As he emerged from the years of silence in 1976, he came into contact with *A Course In Miracles*. Its impact on him was profound. He recognized its unique contribution as a scripture and saw it as the answer to man's urgent need for direct contact with True Knowledge. The Course has been the focal point of his life ever since.

"When I discovered *A Course In Miracles* and read in the Introduction:

Nothing real can be threatened.
Nothing unreal exists.

I recognized the Power of the Word of God in it and also, for the first time, my function in life. A direct relationship with the Scribe came into being for which I will forever be grateful. One is grateful for what is timeless — forever the strength and light of your life. This benediction is your constant companion.

"You realize there is nothing to achieve, perfection is ever complete. God's Plan for Salvation is already accomplished.[4] The truth of this is what brings learning . . . *almost to its appointed end.*[5]

"The wise, it is said, remains ever the stranger to doubt and despair."

The Foundation for Life Action, a federally approved, nonprofit, educational foundation, begun in 1980 on the principles of rightness, virtue and having something to give, started with no money and the conviction not to seek or live off donations. It came to self-reliance by doing workshops and retreats throughout the country, sharing mostly the principles of *A Course In Miracles,* providing an atmosphere of friendship and one-to-one relationship. The Foundation was earning approximately $1000 a day from workshops, retreats, and sales of books and tapes when, at the end of 1982, Tara Singh realized that in order to bring *A Course In Miracles* into application, something other was required than mere workshops and retreats. They had served their purpose.

Since Easter, 1983, Mr. Singh has conducted the Non-Commercialized Retreat: A Serious Study of

A Course In Miracles — an unprecedented, in-depth exploration of the Course at no tuition charge.

"At the height of prosperity, the decision was made to end workshops and retreats and to begin the non-commercialized action — probably the first time it has been offered in the New World. I was told that the Course is to be lived and spent a hundred days to discover intimately what is entailed in bringing it into application. I realized that the Name of God cannot be commercialized. It is something you receive while you give, and fulfills the law that one must teach in order to learn. How can the energy of love be sold?"

Mr. Singh has chosen to work closely on a one-to-one basis with serious students. The program is sponsored by the Foundation for Life Action.

"For the past three and a half years, *A Course In Miracles* has been shared non-commercially. It is a one-to-one, intimate atmosphere where the "Given" is made accessible. But it is for those having the energy of the first thought. For us the student is one whose first love is God.

"The School at *The Branching of the Road* is in the spirit of the Upanishads and the wise men of ancient India and China — where the Teacher and the student lived together and wisdom was neither bought nor sold. The only requirement was a student with the capacity to receive.

Self honesty and the passion to know the
truth of man, God and creation were essential, as well as having no unwillingness
that blocks and evades the holy instant.

Philosophers, educators, gurus —
the interpreters of knowledge —
and others who share their ideas and beliefs,
want to conform us to think in a certain way.

I do not fall into any of these categories.
For me, religious life
is not a concept or a dogma.
It is a state of being.

Absolute Knowledge cannot be interpreted.
It transcends learning.
We can be made aware
of the limitations of our conditioning
and can question our conclusions,
the fallacy of external authority,
as well as our faith in insecurity.

All of this is still in the realm of thought,
adjustments and changes of attitude.
As long as there is relative knowledge,
conflict remains our lot
and we are ever unfulfilled.

It is Undoing by which man is awakened
from the illusion of learning
and the preoccupation
with accumulating information.
Undoing,
by which the awakening can take place,
is of your own energy,
your own internal clarity.

Teaching and learning
are not what the School
at *The Branching of the Road* is about.
The School is for those
who come not to *learn* but to *be*.
There is no authority.
It is consistent with
''. . . where two or more gather
in His Name. . .''[6]
to jointly explore and undo past knowing.
The School is for those
who refuse to be influenced by another
and realize that only the newness within man
can transform his life.

It takes great wisdom and integrity
to come to a silent mind,
to dispel the insanity of helplessness.
True Knowledge is free of conflict
and acknowledges no problem as real.

I am not here to persuade the student
to think in a particular way,
or to give instructions,
or to conform anyone to any ideals.
The School is based on
dissolving misperception.
We do not direct the student
to follow a certain thought system
or a method of solving problems.

The student must be highly responsible
to be a participant
of the one-to-one relationship of the School
to realize the clarity
that frees one from dependence.

*Forgive us our illusions, Father, and
help us to accept our true relationship with You, in which there are no
illusions, and where none can ever
enter.*[7]

"What we share — impart — is Self-
Reliance. To come to Self-Reliance is essential, especially at this time when the
monetary system of the world is in control
of the lives of men. Since man has lost his
work, he has become subject to jobs. Now
he must find his own inner calling and
come to intrinsic work. The Foundation
for Life Action provides a productive life
of intrinsic work where one can come to
Self-Reliance by having something to give
to the world. We undertake to live by
Holy Relationship to discover the Self that
is not a body. To know:

I am sustained by the love of God.[8]

is our undertaking — to forgive and not to
judge as a process of self learning. It is an
internal action since wisdom begins with
the knowledge of self."

Tara Singh is the author of numerous books and
has been featured on many video and audio tapes
in which he discusses the action of bringing one's
life into order, freeing oneself from past conditioning, living the principles of *A Course In Miracles* and
coming to inner awakening.

His life is dedicated to:

"I will not be dishonest to myself"
and to the fact that the Name of God cannot be
commercialized. His thought system is not of lack.
He has no goals, therefore, no doubt.

"God's Plan for Salvation represents
humanity. It is not a religion or an organization. Its purpose is to come to inner
peace."

In answer to the question, "What kind of life do
you envision for yourself?" Tara Singh responded:

"Rightness."

Rightness is independent of personality
and its consequences.
It stands vertical — a law unto itself.
Nothing of the body senses can affect
or obscure it.
Rightness is independent
of the limitations of right and wrong,
thus free of judgment and conflict,
free of lack, of seeking and trying,
free of thought, feelings and reactions.

Such a man is liberated
from the illusion of time
and its beliefs and concepts.
Ever stable, stately and uninvolved,
he knows no loss, gain, or unfulfillment..
Such a man is an extension
of the Grace of God.
He has an atmosphere of purity
surrounding him.
It is a blessing to be in his presence

and to have the ears to hear
his eternal Words.''

The Purpose
Of The
Foundation For Life Action

The purpose of the Foundation for Life Action
is to be with the Eternal Laws
so that it does not become an organization.

LOVE IS ETERNAL.
ABILITIES EXTENDING LOVE ARE BLESSED.

In the absence of Love
abilities become the bondage of skills,
limited to personality.
Among virtuous men,
it is what the human being IS that is Real,
and not what he does in a body.

The purpose of the Foundation is to be part of

GOD'S PLAN FOR SALVATION.[9]

Thus it has a different point of reference
than the thought system of man.

Obviously, the Name of God
cannot be commercialized.
There are no fees in what we share.
We do not believe in loss and gain.
Non-commercialized action is provided by
the blessings of productive life.

"IN GOD WE TRUST"

Those who are with the Eternal Laws
in times of change remain unaffected.
In crisis, it is your care for another
that is your strength.

We have a function in the world
to be truly helpful to others,
knowing:

> *I am sustained by the Love of God.*[10]

> *My only function is the one God gave me.*[11]

> *Nothing real can be threatened.*
> *Nothing unreal exists.*[12]

We are not pressured by the brutality of success.
We are blessed by the work we do.
Gratefulness is complete, as love is independent.

To us, you, the human being, comes first.
Thus it enables us to go past
the conventional opinion of right and wrong
and relate directly to you.

For man is as God created him,
unchanged by the changeable society
that rules his body with its belief systems.

The Truth is a Fact that dissolves illusions of time.
Our function is to dispel the abstraction of ideas
and realize the actuality of Fact.

For,

> *I am under no laws but God's.*[13]

Reverence for Life is of a still mind
hallowed by His Love.

This transformation is what we call

THE PATH OF VIRTUE.

The Path of Virtue is the ministry of gratefulness.

The wise who extends the Kingdom of God on earth lives consistent with,

"BUT SEEK YE FIRST THE KINGDOM OF GOD,
AND HIS RIGHTEOUSNESS;
AND ALL THINGS SHALL BE ADDED UNTO YOU." [14]

References

Introduction

1. *A Course In Miracles* consists of three volumes: *Text, Workbook For Students* and *Manual For Teachers*. The *Text* sets forth the concepts on which the thought system of the Course is based. The *Workbook For Students*, three hundred and sixty-five lessons, is designed to make possible the application of the concepts presented in the *Text*. The *Manual For Teachers* provides answers to some of the basic questions a student of the Course might ask and defines many of the terms used in the *Text*.(Editor)
2. *A Course In Miracles* (ACIM), *Text* (I), page 24.
3. Refers to Matthew 13:13-17.
4. See ACIM, I, page 444.
5. Acts 3:6.
6. ACIM, *Workbook For Students* (II), page 239.
7. ACIM, I, page 444.
8. ACIM, I, page 7.
9. ACIM, I, Introduction.

Statement Of The Participants
Of The One Year Non-Commercialized Retreat

10. ACIM, II, page 53.

PART I

1. *The Gifts Of God*, Foundation for Inner Peace, 1982, page 81.

Chapter 1
Basic Premise Of *A Course In Miracles*
2. ACIM, I, page 275.
3. ACIM, I, page 276.
4. ACIM, II, page 225.
5. ACIM, I, Introduction.
6. ACIM, II, page 58.

Chapter 2
A Course In Miracles — How It Came About
7. Luke 1:38.
8. ACIM, I, page 137.
9. ACIM, I, page 87.
10. ACIM, I, Introduction.

Chapter 3
A Course In Miracles — A Need For Reverence
11. For example, see Matthew 13:13-17.
12. John 13:34.

Chapter 4
Reading *A Course In Miracles*
13. ACIM, II, page 78.
14. ACIM, II, page 229.
15. ACIM, II, page 2.
16. ACIM, II, page 166.

Chapter 5
The Daily Lesson Is Your Daily Bread Of Truth
17. ACIM, II, page 51.
18. Ibid.
19. ACIM, II, page 119.
20. ACIM, I, page 258.
21. ACIM, I, page 123.

PART II
1. *The Gifts Of God*, page 19.

Chapter 6
A Course In Miracles — A New Way Of Life

2. ACIM, I, page 430.
3. ACIM, I, page 320.
4. ACIM, I, Introduction.
5. ACIM, I, page 418.
6. ACIM, II, page 376.
7. ACIM, II, page 392.
8. ACIM, II, page 13.
9. ACIM, II, page 15.
10. ACIM, I, page 464.
11. ACIM, II, page 471.
12. ACIM, I, page 109 .

Chapter 7
A Course In Miracles —
A Response To The Sorrow Of Man
13. ACIM, II, page 162.
14. ACIM, II, page 329.
15. ACIM, II, page 331.
16. ACIM, II, page 334.
17. Ibid.
18. Ibid.
19. The one commandment given by Jesus, ''Love ye one another,'' appears many times in the New Testament. See, for example: John 13:34, 15:12, 15:17; Romans 13:8.
20. ACIM, II, page 334.
21. ACIM, II, page 336.
22. ACIM, II, page 339.
23. Ibid.
24. ACIM, II, page 340.

Chapter 8
A Course In Miracles And Religion
25. ACIM, II, page 353.

Chapter 9
A Course In Miracles Versus Relative Knowledge
26. ACIM, II, page 399.
27. ACIM, I, page 24.

15. ACIM, II, page 376.
16. ACIM, II, page 216.

Chapter 14
What Prevents Application? Unwillingness
17. ACIM, I, pages 354-355.
18. ACIM, III, page 10.
19. ACIM, II, page 274.
20. John 14:12.
21. ACIM, I, page 356.

PART IV
1. *The Gifts Of God*, page 59.

Chapter 15
The Teacher Of God
2. ACIM, III, page 3.
3. While ''siddhi'' literally means accomplishment, it also refers to the attainment of occult or super-normal powers.
4. ACIM, III, page 3.
5. ACIM, II, page 384.
6. Ibid.
7. ACIM, III, page 3.
8. ACIM, I, page 285.

Chapter 16
The Voice Of The Ego
9. ACIM, I, page 37.
10. ACIM, II, page 48.
11. ACIM, II, page 49.
12. Ibid.
13. ACIM, II, page 48.
14. ACIM, II, page 43.
15. ACIM, II, page 18.
16. ACIM, I, page 54.
17. ACIM, II, page 32.
18. ACIM, I, page 255.

19. ACIM, I, page 94.

20. ACIM, I, page 70.

Chapter 17
Forgiveness

21. ACIM, II, page 213.

22. ACIM, II, page 210.

23. ACIM, I, page 42.

24. ACIM, II, page 421.

25. ACIM, III, page 81.

26. Ibid.

27. ACIM, II, page 103.

28. ACIM, II, page 123.

29. ACIM, II, page 103.

30. ACIM, I, page 326.

Chapter 18
The Real World

31. ACIM, I, page 14.

32. ACIM, II, page 451.

33. John 1:1.

34. ACIM, I, page 37.

35. ACIM, I, page 95.

36. ACIM, I, page 45.

37. ACIM, I, pages 88-89.

38. ACIM, I, page 270.

39. ACIM, I, page 207.

40. Ibid.

41. ACIM, I, page 175.

42. ACIM, II, page 79.

43. ACIM, I, page 7.

44. ACIM, I, page 126.

45. ACIM, II, page 469.

Chapter 19
Holy Relationship

46. ACIM, I, page 445.

47. ACIM, I, page 450.

48. Refers to Matthew 13:13-17.

49. ACIM, II, page 476.
50. ACIM, I, page 24.
51. Refers to the Author of *A Course In Miracles*. See ACIM, I, page 6.
52. ACIM, II, page 476.

PART V

1. *The Gifts Of God,* page 3.

Chapter 20
To Be With One's Function
2. ACIM, I, page 306.
3. ACIM, II, page 321.
4. ACIM, II, page 274.
5. ACIM, I, page 287.
6. ACIM, I, page 284.
7. ACIM, II, page 277.
8. ACIM, I, page 302.
9. ACIM, II, page 162.

Chapter 21
What Is Of The Spirit
10. ACIM, II, page 63.
11. ACIM, II, page 223.

PART VI

1. *The Gifts Of God,* page 16.

Chapter 22
Working With *A Course In Miracles* —
''I Need But Call And You Will Answer Me.''
2. ACIM, II, page 119.
3. ACIM, II, page 162.
4. ACIM, II, page 455.
5. Ibid.

Chapter 23
Working With *A Course In Miracles* —
"Let Not My Mind Deny The Thought Of God."

    6. ACIM, II, page 306.

    7. Ibid.

    8. ACIM, II, page 274.

    9. ACIM, II, page 306.

    10. Ibid.

    11. Ibid.

    12. Ibid.

    13. ACIM, II, pages 306-307.

    14. ACIM, II, page 307.

    15. Ibid.

    16. Ibid.

    17. Ibid.

Chapter 24
Working With *A Course In Miracles* —
"I Am Under No Laws But God's."

    18. ACIM, II, page 132.

    19. Ibid.

    20. Ibid.

    21. ACIM, II, page 133.

    22. John 14:12.

    23. Luke 23:34.

Chapter 25
Working With *A Course In Miracles* —
"Today I Claim The Gifts Forgiveness Gives."

    24. ACIM, II, page 459.

    25. ACIM, II, page 3.

    26. ACIM, II, page 162.

    27. ACIM, II, page 459.

    28. Ibid.

    29. ACIM, II, page 18.

    30. Ibid.

31. Ibid.
32. ACIM, II, page 438.
33. ACIM, II, page 18.

Chapter 26
Working With *A Course In Miracles* —
"Peace To My Mind. Let All My Thoughts Be Still."
34. ACIM, II, page 392.
35. Matthew 6:10.
36. ACIM, II, page 392.
37. ACIM, II, page 376.
38. ACIM, II, page 392.
39. Ibid.
40. ACIM, I, Introduction.

PART VII

1. *The Gifts Of God*, page 4.

Chapter 27
Assurances Of Christ — *"You Do Not Walk Alone."*
(NOTE: All references in this chapter are from volume one, the *Text*, of *A Course In Miracles*, except where noted.)
2. ACIM, II, page 478.
3. Page 7.
4. Page 9.
5. Page 12.
6. Page 19.
7. Page 31.
8. Page 35.
9. Page 48.
10. Page 49.
11. Page 49.
12. Page 55.
13. Page 57.
14. Page 62.
15. Page 64.
16. Page 71.
17. Page 76.

18. Page 94.
19. Pages 107-108.
20. Page 109.
21. Page 119.
22. Page 137.
23. Page 151.
24. Pages 179-180.
25. Pages 184-185.
26. Page 187.
27. Page 197.
28. Page 198.
29. Page 204.
30. Page 235.
31. Page 247.
32. Page 248.
33. Page 249.
34. Page 253.
35. Page 259.
36. Page 264.
37. Page 271.
38. Page 279.
39. Page 287.
40. Page 329.
41. Page 353.
42. Pages 353-354.
43. Page 385.
44. Page 393.
45. Page 394.
46. Page 395.
47. Page 404.
48. Page 406.
49. Pages 408-409.
50. Page 425.
51. Pages 429-430.
52. Page 444.
53. Page 446.
54. Page 448.

55. Page 453.
56. Page 454.
57. Page 460.
58. Page 473.
59. Pages 510-511.
60. Page 514.
61. Page 522.
62. Pages 535-536.
63. Page 560.
64. Page 565.
65. Page 568.
66. Page 572.
67. Page 575.
68. Page 588.
69. Page 592.
70. Page 602.
71. Page 604.
72. Page 605.
73. Page 615.
74. Page 621.

ADDENDA

Autobiography Of Tara Singh

1. Refers to ACIM, I, page 444.
2. Refers to Matthew 13:13-17.
3. ACIM, II, page 239.
4. See ACIM, II, page 123.
5. ACIM, II, page 471.
6. Refers to Matthew 18:20.
7. ACIM, I, page 326.
8. ACIM , II, page 79.

Purpose Of The Foundation For Life Action

9. See ACIM, I, pages 426-427; II, page 120 and following.
10. ACIM, II, page 79.
11. ACIM, II, page 107.

12. ACIM, I, Introduction.
13. ACIM, II, page 132.
14. Matthew 6:33.

Guru Nanak ? ⁊ / 8

Other Materials By Tara Singh Related To *A COURSE IN MIRACLES*

BOOKS

A Course In Miracles — A Gift For All Mankind
How To Learn From A Course In Miracles
"Love Holds No Grievances" — The Ending Of Attack
The Future Of Mankind — The Branching Of The Road
How To Raise A Child Of God
Gratefulness

VIDEO CASSETTE TAPES

"Nothing Real Can Be Threatened" —
A Workshop On A Course In Miracles
    Part I   — *The Question And The Holy Instant*
    Part II — *The Deception Of Learning*
    Part III — *Transcending The Body Senses*
    Part IV — *Awakening To Self Knowledge*
Finding Your Inner Calling
How To Raise A Child Of God
Exploring A Course In Miracles (series)
    — *What Is A Course In Miracles*
       and *"The Certain Are Perfectly Calm"*
    — *God Does Not Judge* and *Healing Relationships*
    — *Man's Contemporary Issues*
       and *Life Without Consequences*
    — *Principles* and *Gratefulness*
A Call to Wisdom
       and *A Call To Wisdom — Exploring A Course In Miracles*

Man's Struggle For Freedom From The Past
    and *"Beyond This World There Is A World I Want"*
Life For Life
    and *Moneymaking Is Inconsistent With Life Forces*
The Call To Wisdom: A Discussion On A Course In Miracles
    (Parts I & II)
"Quest Four" with Damien Simpson and Stacie Hunt
"Odyssey" and *"At One With"* with Keith Berwick

AUDIO CASSETTE TAPES

A Course In Miracles Explorations, Series One:
    Origin, Purpose And Application
    (three tape album)
Bringing A Course In Miracles Into Application
    (three tape album)
"What Is The Christ?" (three tape album)
Tara Singh Tapes Of The One Year Non-Commercial-
    ized Retreat: A Serious Study
    Of *A Course In Miracles*

Additional copies of *Commentaries On A Course In Miracles* by Tara Singh may be obtained by sending a check, Mastercard or Visa number and expiration date to:

FOUNDATION FOR LIFE ACTION
902 South Burnside Avenue
Los Angeles, CA 90036
213/933-5591
Toll Free 1/800/732-5489
(Calif.)1/800/367-2246

Limited edition , hardbound $ 16.95
Softcover $ 12.95
(plus $1.75 shipping/handling)

California residents please add 6 1/2% sales tax.

Thank you.

Design: Lucille Frappier and Clio Dixon
Color consultant: Michael Myers
Typesetting: Photographics Inc., Los Angeles, California
Printing/binding: McNaughton & Gunn, Inc., Saline, Michigan
Type: Palacio
Paper: 55lb Glatfelter natural (acid free)